Emotional Intelligence

Unlock the Secrets to Boosting Your EQ, Social Skills, Charisma, Influence and Self Awareness, Including Highly Effective Communication Tips for Persuading People

© **Copyright 2019**

All Rights Reserved. No part of this book may be reproduced in any form without permission in writing from the author. Reviewers may quote brief passages in reviews.

Disclaimer: No part of this publication may be reproduced or transmitted in any form or by any means, mechanical or electronic, including photocopying or recording, or by any information storage and retrieval system, or transmitted by email without permission in writing from the publisher.

While all attempts have been made to verify the information provided in this publication, neither the author nor the publisher assumes any responsibility for errors, omissions or contrary interpretations of the subject matter herein.

This book is for entertainment purposes only. The views expressed are those of the author alone, and should not be taken as expert instruction or commands. The reader is responsible for his or her own actions.

Adherence to all applicable laws and regulations, including international, federal, state and local laws governing professional licensing, business practices, advertising and all other aspects of doing business in the US, Canada, UK or any other jurisdiction is the sole responsibility of the purchaser or reader.

Neither the author nor the publisher assumes any responsibility or liability whatsoever on the behalf of the purchaser or reader of these materials. Any perceived slight of any individual or organization is purely unintentional.

Contents

INTRODUCTION 1

CHAPTER 1: EMOTIONS AND INTELLIGENCE 3

CHAPTER 2: EMOTIONAL INTELLIGENCE IS ANOTHER FORM OF MIND 8

CHAPTER 3: WHERE DID THE EMOTIONS COME FROM? 15

CHAPTER 4: FIVE KEY SKILLS FOR DEVELOPING EMOTIONAL INTELLIGENCE 20

CHAPTER 5: AMPLIFIER OF EMOTIONS OF JOY – A RESOURCE THAT IS ALWAYS WITH YOU 28

CHAPTER 6: ANGER MANAGEMENT – EMOTIONAL RESILIENCE IN CONFLICT 36

CHAPTER 7: MANAGING FEAR, AND HOW TO DEVELOP COURAGE 42

CHAPTER 8: SELF-CONFIDENCE – THE PATH FROM UNCERTAIN SELF-ESTEEM TO RELIABLE SELF-WORTH 47

CHAPTER 9: LAUGHTER ANATOMY – HOW TO DEVELOP A SENSE OF HUMOR 56

CHAPTER 10: SORROW – THE ANTIDOTE FOR DEPRESSION 62

CHAPTER 11: INSPIRATION – WHERE IS YOUR ENTHUSIASM "START" BUTTON? 67

CHAPTER 12: INFECTED WITH A SENSE OF GUILT 73

CHAPTER 13: ANATOMY OF THE FEELING OF RESENTMENT – THE RECIPE FOR RADICAL FORGIVENESS 81

CHAPTER 14: JEALOUSY 90

CHAPTER 15: POISONOUS EMOTIONS 95

CHAPTER 16: IMPROVING EMOTIONAL CONSCIOUSNESS 100

CONCLUSION 108

Introduction

Emotional intelligence is something within each of us that we are barely conscious of. Something that determines how we control our behavior, how we present ourselves in society, how we communicate with other people, and how we make decisions.

Emotional intelligence helps us to know about an influence on our emotions and those of others; an ability that allows us to reduce stress, learn to communicate effectively, overcome obstacles, and resolve conflicts. Emotional intelligence should be integral in most of our everyday activities. Its mastery will influence our attitudes and our attitudes to those around us positively. Anyone who has the skill of high emotional intelligence is able to determine their emotional state and that of those around They know how to attract people without any manipulation and deception and they are just someone with whom people heartily want to follow or spend time with.

Why is a high emotional quotient (EQ) considered so important? Because those who are not the most "outstanding" people in certain areas often turn out to be more successful in work or happier in their personal lives. You probably know people brilliantly educated and yet socially disordered, unlucky in business, and unsuccessful in personal relationships. High IQ (intelligence quotient, intelligence coefficient) is not enough to be happy and successful in all areas of life—in any case, in those areas that are the most important to us. IQ will help to enter university, but EQ (emotional quotient, emotional coefficient) testifies to our ability to cope in many different capacities. IQ can help you get a job interview, but things like getting into a team and building relationships are the responsibility of EQ.

You will not only read in this book about what constitutes emotional intelligence in action, but also: how you can develop and use it, and how it will help you solve some problems and prevent others. You will discover for yourself how to have a high EQ and reach a level of emotional equilibrium, and use your new self-awareness to find success in all of the most important areas of life.

Chapter 1: Emotions and Intelligence

Emotional intelligence is a concept that has emerged in addition to intelligence in its traditional sense. If we usually associate intelligence with such things as the mind, education, and IQ level, then emotional intelligence is something else. This is a person's ability to perceive and use emotional information that is received, or transmitted, through emotions. Emotional intelligence is included in the range of interests of both the natural sciences and the humanities—neurology, psychology, neuropsychology, physiology, sociology, and philosophy.

Often, hearing about emotional intelligence, people ask themselves whether it can even be called "intelligence." Emotions are informative, just control your own communication to see this. You will notice that most of the information you receive is not from the person's words, but from the expression on their face. When it comes to first impressions, many people often feel that they immediately understand whether a person is kind of "evil," or "honest," or if they are not trustworthy. This is called the ability to communicate and establish contact, and at a more advanced level—the ability to understand people. And it's always about emotions.

Emotions are subjective states experienced by humans and animals; emotions arise in response to the influence of external or internal stimuli and appear in the form of direct experiences—for example, pleasure or displeasure, joy, fear, and anger.

Although we are talking about "fear in the heart" and "joy in the soul," emotions are born in the brain due to the activation of its corresponding structures. A long time ago, experiments showed that the excitation of certain structures in the brain causes the appearance of positive emotions, which the body seeks to strengthen, extend, or repeat. On the contrary, the excitation of other structures leads to the appearance of negative emotions, which the body seeks to eliminate or weaken. Hence the biological significance of emotions: they have an evaluative function, thanks to which the body can respond in advance and quickly to environmental changes, to mobilize the necessary energy to satisfy immediate needs. This means that emotions are filled with certain information, and their appearance is also due to specific reasons because emotions do not arise without a trigger. They are always a response to the stimuli—the environment, the event.

Emotions do not just remain in the background as life flows by; they directly affect attitudes and relationships, and they participate in the most important process for a person—decision making. It is often said that emotions interfere with making decisions, but this is debatable: emotions motivate, and a motivated person is inclined to make decisions based on those emotions. A decision may be wrong; just as a decision made unemotionally may turn out to be wrong. So that emotions do not fail, emotional intelligence must be developed—just as a person develops the mind.

Emotions underlie an individual's life experience. Playing the role of negative or positive reinforcement, they help to develop, consolidate, and preserve particliar forms of behavior, or, conversely, to eliminate them. If this reminded you of the experiments of the academic Ivan Pavlov, you are right. The most famous were his experiments on dogs: after a bell rang, the dog was given food—at the sight of which it literally began to drool. Subsequently, when the bell rang, the dog's saliva began to be produced in advance: the animal now associated the sound of the bell ringing with eating tasty food. Now think of your own emotional reactions to various stimuli. For example, when you are waiting for a call from a person dear to you, you are likely to grab the phone with hope and joy every time that it rings. And vice versa: if someone you don't want to hear from calls you, the phone call will cause dread and other unpleasant emotions.

It's a big mistake to think that emotions are too vague, biased, or uncontrollable. The development of emotions is a crucial step on the evolutionary path, which is confirmed by the opinion of the founder of the theory of evolution. Charles Darwin said that emotions help evaluate incoming information (for example, the degree of danger) and, as a result, we choose the line of behavior that we deem is the most suitable for a given situation.

It turns out that emotions also serve us as a means of increasing reliability and expanding the adaptive capabilities of the body. Having an emotional response is also one of the main ways that human's internally regulate their mental activity and behavior.

It must be understood that emotions—and we will also mention this in one of the sections of the book—are to a large extent (like actions) determined by the norms of morality and law where we live. Such "norms" exist in every society (even if in some environments, moral and legal norms are such that we cannot force ourselves to consider them moral and correct). This is very easy to notice when communicating with representatives of different cultures: the Japanese, for example, are extremely restrained in expressing their emotions. The Japanese will not reveal their souls to you nor talk freely about the details of their life. But, here in the USA, it is quite normal to express emotions openly and this is often found even among complete strangers: in line, on a train, in a hospital.

Emotions appear to help satisfy certain needs, but the connection is not limited to this: spiritual, aesthetic, moral, and intellectual needs are also the basis for the emergence of feelings—the highest forms of emotions.

What is accompanied by the emergence of any person's needs? If you think carefully, then the answer will be: the emergence of any need, without exception, is always accompanied by a feeling of dissatisfaction, which intensifies with any unsuccessful attempt to satisfy the need (that is, when the efforts do not reach the goal). This is a very good demonstration of the need for love: the more negative love experiences a person has, the sharper the feeling of dissatisfaction and the stronger the need for love. The emotions that accompany such experiences can only be imagined: perhaps anger, resentment, hatred, self-loathing and despair.

So we come to the fact that emotions are positive or negative. Nature has decreed that we do not experience only positive emotions. They fulfill their biological task: since negative emotions accompany an unmet need, they encourage a person to overcome obstacles that impede the satisfaction of their needs. In other words, take a closer look at this seemingly paradoxical fact: if we hadn't been "so bad," we would not have known that we were "so bad" and would not have tried to change anything. If we did not feel hunger, we would not have the need to eat and very soon we would reach an extreme degree of exhaustion, and subsequently die.

Satisfying our needs leads to positive emotions. In this state, we have a feeling of satisfaction, happiness, enjoyment, joy, and gratitude—not only as the result of our efforts but also as a reward for our work. With their help, the body confirms that we tried not in vain and that getting what is vital is both useful and simply pleasant. Biologically positive emotions help the body to assess the degree of satisfaction of its needs. They are associated with the so-called sensory saturation mechanisms which are widely represented in the processes of satisfying different needs (in food, in communication, in proximity, etc.). Moreover, when a person is methodically trained to satisfy one and the same need, he acquires the ability to be guided to achieve the goal not only by negative emotions, but also by ideas about those positive emotions that will appear when the need is satisfied. So a person begins to look for pleasure: they know from their experience that a certain action will give them a lot of positive emotions.

The most obvious examples are food and sex, and these examples are indicative because they are reminiscent of extremes: in the pursuit of satisfying a need and receiving positive emotions, a person runs the risk of becoming dependent on this satisfaction. Therefore, these feelings unchecked, produce gluttons or the highest order of Casanova (male or female).

Chapter 2: Emotional Intelligence is Another Form of Mind

The study of emotional intelligence began in 1937, when hereditary psychologist Robert Thorndike published work on social intelligence. In 1940, the outstanding psychologist David Wechsler (who was also influenced by Thorndike's father) advanced the topic with an article on intellectual and non-intellectual components. Wechsler pointed out that non-intellectual components are even more important for social adaptation than intellectual ones. It was with them that a serious study of this phenomenon began. An important milestone was also in 1983 when Howard Gardner wrote about "multiple intelligences", and 1990, when American psychologists John Mayer and Peter Salovey introduced the term "emotional intelligence" and began a research program to measure it. We'll definitely mention Daniel Goleman's book "Emotional Intelligence," which was published in 1995 and has become a classic: despite the fact that the term itself was not his idea.

Mayer and Salovey coined the phrase "emotional intelligence". Scientists have described EQ based on its constituent parts. Emotional intelligence is a combination of four skills, among which we have:

• The accuracy of evaluating and expressing emotions: the ability to determine emotions according to their physical state and thoughts, appearance, and behavior. This also includes the ability to express your emotions and related needs to other people.

• The use of emotions in mental activity: an understanding of how you can think more effectively using emotions. Many problems come from the fact that some people do not know how to control their emotions, do not understand them, and are not able to control them. If a person has such a skill, they gain an invaluable gift—the ability to stand in another's position, look at themselves from this side, and evaluate the situation from different points of view. All this is the ability to see the world from different angles. This skill is extremely productive, because it allows you to regulate relationships and find solutions to pressing problems.

• Understanding of emotions: the ability to determine the source of emotions, classify them, recognize the relationship between words and emotions, interpret the meanings of emotions related to relationships, understand complex feelings, be aware of transitions from one emotion to another. Researchers include here the possible further development of emotion.

• Managing emotions: the ability to use the information that they give, evoke emotions or move away from them (depending on their information content or usefulness), manage others' emotions and your own.

EQ, fortunately, can be developed. This is not what is given to us from birth and for life. Although, for example, J. Mayer believes that it is impossible to increase the level of emotional intelligence, because, in his opinion, this is just a given. But then he admits that through training, a person can increase their level of emotional competence—the ability to recognize their feelings and the feelings of other people with the goals of self-motivation and controlling their emotions.

Among his opponents, we see a very authoritative D. Goleman, a true titan in the study of emotional intelligence. Goleman believes that emotional intelligence can be developed because the nerve pathways of the brain continue to develop until the middle of human life. The methods of developing emotional intelligence can be very different, and among them, everyone will find at least one that is most suitable: family education, relationships in society, close relationships with the opposite sex, and simply life experience itself, which, as you know, is the best teacher.

When studies of emotional intelligence became widely available, they turned out to be the missing link in regard to a specific question: why do people with average intelligence (IQ) get ahead of competitors with the highest intelligence seventy percent of the time? This problem cast a dense shadow on what people had always mistaken for the only main requirement for being successful: IQ. Conversely, several pieces of research all agree that emotional intelligence is also as important as this other mostly focused on component of intelligence.

Emotional intelligence consists of three basic skills that describe personal and social understanding:

1.) Personal skill: consists of our self-awareness and self-management skills. This focuses on us as a person and not much on our interactions with others. This involves being able to understand our current state and emotions and being able to control our inclinations and behavior. Two skills belong to it:

a.) Self-awareness – this involves being able to accurately feel our present emotions and track their appearance and development. We are aware of our personal emotions, the way they affect our thinking and behavioral patterns, we know our strong points and our weak points, and maintain self-confidence; and b.) Self-government – the ability to use an understanding of one's emotions in order to remain flexible and positively direct one's behavior. We are able to manage sudden actions or impulsive feelings in healthy ways, and to manage our emotions, think and act the right way, fulfill obligations, and adapt to changing circumstances.

2.) Social competence: consists of understanding the processes taking place in our environment and of our understanding of human relations and relationships. This aspect is involved in our understanding of the moods of those around us, their present behavior and the reasons for such behavior, in order to enhance the quality of the relationship between us and other people. This also includes two skills:

a.) Social understanding – the ability to accurately notice the emotions of other people and understand what is really happening. Thanks to this skill, we identify and come to an understanding of the emotions, problems, and needs of others, and how to feel comfortable in society; and

b.) Relationship management – the ability to use an understanding of one's and other's emotions to manage interactions with other people successfully. We know how to start and continue with (in a healthy way) good relationships, how to speak in such a way that we are not misunderstood, inspire others, how to work well with a host of others and find a way out of conflict situations.

Emotional intelligence and IQ are two different things. Emotional intelligence is a fundamental element of human behavior that is distinct from intelligence. There is no known connection between a measure of intelligence and emotional intelligence; it is completely impossible to predict the level of emotional intelligence based on how smart someone is—that is, how high their IQ is. IQ itself is misunderstood as a degree of education or as an indicator of genius. IQ in itself is your ability to learn, and at fifteen you have the same IQ as at fifty. Emotional intelligence, on the other hand, is not a fixed gift. You can learn how to develop it. Also, with constant learning, use, and practice, you can be a master of emotional intelligence. Of course, some people naturally have higher emotional intelligence than others, but you can develop emotional intelligence to a high level if you wish, even if you had no idea that you could.

3.) Individuality: the last piece of the mosaic. Individuality is the result of deep preferences, such as a tendency to focus on oneself or, conversely, to display extroverted behavior. However, like IQ, personality cannot be used to predict the level of emotional intelligence. Like IQ, personality is stable and does not change throughout life. IQ, emotional intelligence, and individuality—each of these phenomena represents a unique basis for the interaction of a person with themselves and with the world around him.

Emotional intelligence affects:

• Our success at work – Emotional intelligence helps to manage contacts, which is especially important if a person is working in a team or if his work is related to communication (and the vast majority of classes are suitable for these criteria). EQ helps to motivate people, and if there is an element of competition in work, to surpass rivals.

• Physical health – Modern life is stressful; it is a fact. Of course, there are people who have less stress, but in general, it is not about who has more or who has less, but how much a person is able to manage it. If you are unable to control the level of stress, this can lead to serious health problems. Uncontrolled stress can suppress the immune system, increase the risk of a heart attack, raise blood pressure, contribute to infertility, and accelerate the aging process. Therefore, a vital prerequisite to developing and improving your EQ is to try to find out and understand how to reduce stress.

• Mental health – Consistent stress can also affect a person's mental health, making them susceptible to depression and anxiety. When we are unable to understand and respond properly to our emotions, we find ourselves subject to mood changes, and the inability to control ourselves leads to the inability to form strong relationships, which in the end can make us experience acute loneliness.

• Relationships – Understanding our emotions and knowing how to respond properly to them, we are able to express our feelings better, we understand what other people feel, and how. This skill allows us to interact better and more efficiently and create better relationships both at work and in our personal life.

So, emotional intelligence is associated with success at work. Think about how much your emotional intelligence affects professional success. The short answer is: very much, because it is a powerful way to focus energy in one direction with a huge result. During a large-scale study comparing emotional intelligence with thirty-three other skills important for work, social psychologists from the Aristotle University of Thessaloniki found that it was emotional intelligence that is the strongest predictor of success at work—and it determines fifty-eight percent of success, and in all professional areas. More than half! And it turns out that such important factors as IQ, education profile, previous experience, etc. account for even less than half of the merits.

Our emotional intelligence is the basis for acquiring the most important skills, and it is critical because it affects most of what we say and do every day. EQ is the most important criterion for success in the workplace, and for those who aim at a high position, this is the most important factor in leadership.

Among the study participants were executives, including large international companies; it turned out that ninety percent of them had a very high level of emotional intelligence. At the same time, only twenty percent of employees holding grassroots positions had a highly developed emotional intelligence, which means that sooner or later, they will be considered to occupy a much higher position. If others develop their emotional intelligence, their capabilities will also improve remarkably. You can be the top person working for a company without emotional intelligence, but the chances are small.

Emotional intelligence can be developed. This is certainly its most encouraging property. The communication between our emotional and rational "brains" is the physical source of emotional intelligence. The pathway for emotional intelligence begins in the brain; when an event involving us occurs, our primary feelings arise here and through the limbic system break through to the forefront of the brain before we can rationally think about what has happened. So, we have an emotional reaction to events before the mind is able to comprehend them. Emotional intelligence, therefore, requires effective communication between the rational and emotional centers of the brain.

There is such a term—"neuroplasticity." Neurologists use it to describe the brain's ability to change. The brain grows new connections when we learn new skills. Changes gradually occur because brain cells develop new connections to accelerate the effectiveness of newly acquired skills. Using strategies for developing emotional intelligence allows billions of microscopic neurons that pave the road between the rational and emotional centers of the brain to "pull branches" to reach other cells. One cell can grow fifteen thousand bonds with neighbors. When we train our brains constantly using new strategies to increase our emotional intelligence, emotionally intelligent behavior becomes a habit.

Chapter 3: Where Did the Emotions Come From?

If a few pages ago, we remembered Charles Darwin, then we simply have no right to forget about evolution. In terms of evolution, the source of emotions can be considered as primary forms of irritability. But true emotions are associated with the development of special brain structures, primarily limbic formations. Thanks to these formations, the transition of the active nature of behavior to a qualitatively new level has occurred. The brain has acquired the ability to use subjective experiences (that is, emotions) of one's own state as a stimulating and driving force of behavior.

The first physiological theory of the emergence of emotions is the so-called peripheral theory. It was proposed by William James and Carl Lange in the 1880s. In their opinion, emotions are a consequence of changes in the activity of internal organs and skeletal muscles, and these changes are caused by appropriate stimuli.

This theory has a right to exist, but it is used mainly to explain emotions that are caused by the physical condition of the body (for example, a person is sick and, as a result, experiences a variety of negative emotions). But this theory is not suitable for explaining emotions of a higher level because it is impossible to explain that social or aesthetic emotions are caused by changes in internal organs. If possible, it is only a stretch, like structural changes in the brain that lead to psychopathologies and, accordingly, some social (or antisocial) sensations.

In the first third of the twentieth century, the so-called Cannon—Bard (or thalamic) theory of Walter Cannon and Philip Bard was put forward. This theory is based on the fact that in a certain structure of the brain—the thalamus—emotional excitations are formed, resulting in reactions to the periphery of the brain that are characteristic of a particular emotion. Following this, James Papez put forward his theory (the "Papez circuit"), which gives the main role in the formation of emotions to the limbic structures of the brain. Since we previously mentioned the limbic system and promised to devote a special section to it, you realize that it was this scientist who came up with the solution. According to his theory, emotional excitations begin and end in the hippocampus—spreading to the mamillary bodies, then through the thalamus to the cingulate gyrus in what is called the Papez circuit. According to Papez, the spread of emotional arousal from the cingulate gyrus to the cortex of the cerebral hemispheres creates an emotional coloring of mental processes.

We talked about the fact that emotions are necessary for us to live and adapt to society. This idea was actively developed in the mid-twentieth century by the physiologist Pyotr Kuzmich Anokhin. He developed a biological theory, which is based on the fact that emotions arose during the process of evolution as a means of more successful adaptation by living beings to the conditions of existence. Emotions were useful for survival and allowed living things to quickly and more economically respond to external influences; leading to emerging internal needs and satisfaction. In addition, emotions allow animals and humans to evaluate the impact on the body of various—including damaging—factors. They produce an almost instantaneous integration of all body functions, as a result of which the usefulness or harmfulness of the influencing factor is determined. Emotions, in fact, track a changing environment and thus help the body to develop a response. Often such a reaction is produced at lightning speed.

We are interested in another theory, the authorship of which also belongs to Pavel V. Simonov. His theory suggests that the emotional state of the body is determined by two factors: on the one hand, negative emotions that accompany the initial needs of the body, and on the other hand, the probable forecasting of positive emotions in meeting these needs. Evaluation by the brain of the two most important factors—the need and the likelihood of its satisfaction—may be a necessary and sufficient condition for the appearance of a spectrum of emotions.

Emotions and the Brain

If emotions appear in response to an external stimulus, a logical question arises: where do they appear? There are certain physiological mechanisms, the knowledge of which helps us to understand where our emotional reactions come from.

The "method of irritation" made it possible to objectify the emotional sensations in animals. It all began in 1954, when two researchers at McGill University, James Olds and Peter Milner, were preparing to conduct electrical stimulation of the reticular formation of the rat brain stem while teaching these animals how to solve problems. Scientists have implanted electrodes in those areas of the brain of animals that are most suitable for the task. In preliminary experiments, the researchers noticed that when the electric pulse was turned on, the rat constantly ran away to a certain place. The more often they observed such an effect, the more the rat intrigued them. Therefore, they decided to automate the methodology in order to study in detail this "forced repetition."

However, the story did not end there. James Olds compiled maps of brain regions from which this effect could be obtained. The technique did not give the expected results, but by a fluke, a part of the brain (the medial anterior brain bundle in the septum) was discovered, which turned out to be one of the main areas for obtaining this effect. The rest of the irritation system extends back from this zone and includes areas of the brain stem.

Experiments using irritation techniques have demonstrated the ability to form drives to repeat electrical stimulation of limbic structures in animals of various species (reptiles, birds, and mammals). This attraction is often quite strong and causes animals to overcome significant obstacles in order to obtain a positive effect. Self-stimulation zones are considered as centers of positive emotions. They are widely represented in the area of the lateral hypothalamus (part of the hypothalamus), the reticular formation of the midbrain, in the septum, tonsil, hippocampus, and other limbic formations. In the cerebral cortex, such zones are much smaller.

Irritation of some brain structures causes pronounced avoidance reactions in animals. These areas of the brain are considered to be zones of negative emotions (or negative zones). Their stimulation causes an extremely negative attitude toward the environment in which irritation was carried out. Therefore, animals are not only afraid to re-enter the veterinary office, where they were once hurt, but they experience the most unpleasant emotions when entering a room associated with some kind of traumatic event. Zones whose irritation causes distinct negative emotional reactions are also located in the hypothalamus, in the central part of the reticular formation of the midbrain and septum, as well as in the tonsil.

Often, people learning that negative emotions are born not just "in the head"—but in well-defined brain structures—indulge in thoughts about the possibility of improving themselves. What if these structures are removed from the brain? Then, after all, the negativity will be taken away, and we will no longer feel resentment, disbelief, doubt, dissatisfaction—is it not so?

Of course, scientists have already asked this question. Reactions in the absence of objective criteria causing emotions, Walter Cannon called "false emotional reactions." Such reactions are observed when the amygdala and hippocampus are removed, and rage too when the cerebral cortex is removed. In other words, the formula "no brain area—no problem" does not work. Emotions remain. Friedrich Goltz in the late 1800s observed dogs that had their cerebral cortex removed. Dogs reacted viciously to any external irritations. Moreover, rage swept them to such an extent that they lost the ability to assess the stimulus adequately; their reaction was excessive, and even dogs that were friendly before the operation attacked their owners after it.

Two other scientists, Heinrich Kluver, and Paul Bucy, found that after monkeys had the temporal regions of the cortex removed, they developed a syndrome (named after the researchers as Kluver-Bucy syndrome): these animals continued to be affected by stimuli, but they no longer evaluated their biological significance. They could not see the danger in what was to cause alarm; for example, they could eat a completely inedible object or continue to grab a lit match even after being burned. They had completely lost their sense of fear, but this was not a condition called fearlessness; on the contrary, the animals became tame, they began to trust absolutely everyone (even those who they would not have trusted before). In addition to this, in their flock, these animals became maladaptive; in other words, unsuitable for a society of their own kind and as a result lost their position in the pack. Researchers have proved that in all cases of damage to the cerebral cortex, emotional reactions become perverted.

Chapter 4: Five Key Skills for Developing Emotional Intelligence

In relation to joy and relative success in life, EQ is thought to mean as much as IQ. A strong EQ helps an individual to develop strong relationships. It also helps to improve work success and helps you better achieve both individual and collective goals. Not to over flog the importance, but it is useful to know how to increase your EQ. Five basic skills will help.

All incoming information approaches the brain through our senses. When this information is radically tense or emotional, the instinct takes over, and our ability to act is limited by the basic skills necessary for survival: running, fighting, or mentally detaching. Therefore, in order to make a choice from a list of "profitable" and socially acceptable options, we must always be able to balance emotions.

Memory is also closely related to emotion. Learning to use the emotional region of our brain in the same way as the rational, we not only expand our range of choices when it comes to our reactions to stimuli; we also learn to engage our emotional memory in decision making. This helps to prevent the continuous repetition of past mistakes. To increase the level of EQ, as we have already hinted, you need to understand the emotional side of your brain and learn how to manage it. The knowledge that you will get from this book will help you with this because this knowledge in itself is a valuable weapon. There are five key skills; having mastered the first two, it will be much easier for you to master the other three.

So, developing emotional intelligence goes through five key skills:

- Skill 1: Quickly reduce stress.

- Skill 2: Understand and manage your emotions.

- Skill 3: Establish contact with others using non-verbal communication.

- Skill 4: Use humor and play to cope with challenges and overcome obstacles.

- Skill 5: Positively resolve conflicts.

Any person can learn these skills at any time, regardless of age or education. But there is a dissimilarity between knowing about your EQ and putting this into practice. Knowing that a certain thing has to be done does not mean that we shall do it. Most often, this is the case when we are overwhelmed by a strain that could negate our best intentions.

A high level of tension can interfere with a person's ability to accurately decode the situation, hear what others are saying, know about their own feelings and needs, clearly express their thoughts, and communicate with others. The ability to quickly calm yourself and reduce stress helps to stay balanced, focused, and control yourself no matter what problems arise or how stressful the situation becomes.

To constantly change and improve your behavior while under emotional stress, you should know how to use to your advantage the powerful emotional parts of the brain that remain active and accessible even during times of intense emotional pressure. This means that you cannot just read about emotional intelligence to master it. You must experience and practice these skills in everyday life. We will talk about how to do this now.

Skill Lesson 1 – How to Reduce Stress

Develop your stress management skills by following these steps:

- Be aware that you are stressed. Recognize that you are under pressure. The preliminary step involves understanding what it means to feel stressed. Control: note how you feel when you are under pressure. How does your body react? Watch how the muscles tighten (note that under stress, they constantly maintain tension),you're your breathing changes (it becomes more superficial and uneven). To be aware of your physical response to stress means to be able to regulate stress when it happens.

- Find your answer to stress. Every person responds to this state in their own way. Those who are inclined to get angry or worried will be best helped by such methods (thoughts, activities) that soothe. Those who are prone to depression will benefit from stimulating actions. Those who become distracted and slow need action that provides both comfort and stimulation.

- Find a stress management technique that is right for you. There are a great many techniques; among them, there is one that will work best for you. Do not despair if the tried and tested methods did not help—you simply did not find yours. Be assured it exists. Neurologists and psychologists around the world have been improving stress management techniques for decades. While you are looking for your way, remember a simple rule: the best way to quickly reduce stress is to turn on at least one of the channels of perception: visual, auditory, olfactory, tactile, and taste. Again, each person responds differently to the activation of the senses, so you need to find things that quickly calm you down or, conversely, invigorate you. For example, if your visual channel works better than others, visuals will help you evoke an emotional response and change your mood for the better (it can be anything from visiting a museum to watching a movie or looking at a magazine). If you are more responsive to sound, turn on music or go to the park and listen to the wind in the tree branches. Find your way!

Skill Lesson 2 – How to Understand and Manage Your Emotions

The key to understanding yourself and others is the ability to be in contact with your emotions, to be aware of them, and to know how they affect your thoughts and actions. It seems so simple, but, unfortunately, some people do not even think that it matters at all. And as a result, many people are disconnected from their emotions, do not feel contact with them, do not know the signs of their appearance and manifestation, and do not know how to control them; this is especially true of strong underlying emotions such as fear, joy, anger, and sadness. Such a disconnection with one's own emotions can be the result of negative events, especially those that took place in childhood, which taught a person to turn off their feelings. But, by distorting or denying our feelings, we cannot eliminate them. They are still within us, whether we know about them or not.

What relationships do you have with your emotions?

- Do your feelings "transcend," as if changing from one emotional level to another? When you have a change of emotions, do you feel it, do you feel how your state is changing?

- Are your emotions accompanied by responses that you experience in your stomach, chest, throat, or on your body (for example, a lump in your throat, tightness in your chest, a change in appetite, or goosebumps, etc.)?

- Do you experience hidden emotions (anger, sadness, fear, joy), each of which is evident in the subtle expressions of your face?

- Can you experience intense feelings that are strong enough to capture both your attention and that of others?

- Do you pay attention to your emotions? Do they influence decision making?

If you are unfamiliar with any of these experiences, your emotions may be diminished or turned off. To be emotionally healthy and emotionally intelligent, you must reconnect with your core emotions, accept them, and feel comfortable in this interaction with them. Emotional understanding can be studied at any time of life. If you do not know how to manage stress, it is important to start with this. When you master this skill, it will become much easier for you to regain contact with your emotional world. You will find it much easier to transfer strong or unpleasant emotions and even change how you feel and respond to them.

Skill Lesson 3 – How to Learn Non-Verbal Communication

To be a good conversationalist, it takes much more than just the ability to speak beautifully. Moreover, very often, how you make a statement is more important and is more noticed than even the statement itself. The non-verbal signs that you portray to the interlocutor are of great importance: tone of voice, facial expressions, gestures, body position (in which position you are sitting or standing, how close you are to the interlocutor), how fast (slow) or how loud (quiet) you speak, and whether you look into the eyes of the person you are talking to. To ensure that you maintain the attention of others and build trusting relationships with them, you must know and control your body language. You should also be able to accurately read and respond to non-verbal messages that other people send you. These messages are not interrupted when a person stops talking. Even when you are silent, you still communicate non-verbally.

Think about what you are broadcasting and how what you transmit is related to what you are feeling. If you insist that everything is fine with you, and at the same time you grit your teeth and look away, your body clearly signals the opposite, that you are not doing well. Your non-verbal messages may give the impression of interest, trust, emotion—or fear, confusion, distrust, and disinterest.

Want to improve your non-verbal communication? Success in this area depends on your ability to control stress, recognize your own emotions, and understand the signals you send and receive. When you chat:

• Focus on your conversation partner. If, instead of concentrating on him (or her), you are absorbed in thoughts about what to say next, or you daydream, or reflect on something else, then be sure that you will not miss non-verbal messages and other subtleties of the conversation;

• Make eye contact. Look into the eyes of the person you are talking to, only periodically looking away for a few seconds so as not to cause tension by staring. Eye contact can convey interest, support the conversation, and help understand the other person's response and his reaction to your words; and

• Pay attention to the non-verbal cues you send and receive, such as facial expressions, tone of voice, body position, gestures, and the pace of the conversation.

Skill Lesson 4 – How to Use Humor and a Game to Cope with Challenges

Humor, laughter, and play are natural antidotes to the difficulties of life. They help to ease the burden and to see something good in what is happening and find hope that it will be better in the future. The joke helps to look at the problem from the other side; it makes it easier to treat it. Laughing heartily is proven to reduce stress, improve mood, and return the nervous system to a state of balance. Fun, playful communication makes the relationship livelier. And in general, humor expands the scope of emotional intelligence, helping us to:

• Overcome obstacles and cope with difficulties. With a sense of humor, we allow ourselves to consider frustration in a new perspective; laughter and play allow us to survive periods of irritation, difficult times, delays in important matters, and unexpected barriers to the goal;

● Smooth corners. Using humorous language, we can easily express that which would otherwise not be possible without such humor;

● Simultaneously relax and stimulate oneself. Communication with the element of the game reduces fatigue and relaxes the body, which allows us to "recharge the batteries;" and

● Show creativity. Relaxing, we free ourselves from the inert thinking style, allowing our thoughts to bring unexpected and fresh ideas, and ourselves to look at things in a new way.

It's not so difficult to develop the ability to communicate easily, while being fun and lively. And most importantly, it's never too late for the conversation to turn into laughter. It's never too late to see for yourself or to show others your play-filled, perky and humorous side. For this you need, firstly, to practice more often: the more you joke and laugh, the easier this becomes. Secondly, you need to find pleasant actions that relax you and help you express your playful nature. And finally, a good way to practice is by playing with animals, young children, and people who value playful banter.

Skill Lesson 5 – How to Positively Resolve Conflicts

Conflict and disagreements are inevitable in a relationship. Two people cannot always have the same needs, opinions, and expectations. However, one must understand that this is normal. Getting a resolution to any issue in a positive way and without hurting either party helps to develop trust between both parties. As soon as the resolution is not deemed as a threat or one that restricts freedoms, then creativity and security are built in relationships. The ability to manage conflicts in a positive, trust-building way is supported by the previous four skills of emotional intelligence. Once you understand how to manage stress, be emotionally conscious, communicate non-verbally, and use humor and play, you will immediately have the means to deal with emotionally charged negative situations, as well as to identify potential conflict situations and discharge them before they explode.

There are several ways to resolve conflicts in a way that will strengthen relationships and build trust between the parties involved:

- Stay focused on the present. Do not cling to old grievances and resentment. This will help you to accept reality, understand the essence of the situation, and not only solve it, but also consider it as a way to get rid of old and unnecessary or conflicting feelings.

- Choose your arguments. Arguments for resolving a conflict require time and energy, especially if you want to resolve it in a positive way. Determine what is worth arguing about and what is not worth the effort.

- Goodbye. Let bygones be bygones. Let the hurtful behavior of others remain in the past. To get a proper resolution, you must first abandon the desire to punish and get revenge.

- Stop conflicts that cannot be resolved. Such conflicts encourage people to continue arguing endlessly. It's easy to distinguish such a conflict: the debate goes on and on, the passions are heating up, and you understand that nothing can be fixed. No one will convince anyone. The goal of the dispute is not the search for truth, but the conflict itself, and over time, everything will only get worse. If you are drawn into a conflict that cannot be resolved, get out of it. Just pull yourself out of it, stop arguing, and stop proving, stop refuting—do it even if you still disagree with the opponent's opinion.

The following chapters discuss a practical course on managing feelings and emotions. By understanding these, you develop your emotional competence and better react to situations. You also rewire yourself to understand the emotions of others and be a better version of yourself.

Chapter 5: Amplifier of Emotions of Joy – A Resource that Is Always with You

> There are three traps that steal joy: regret for the past, anxiety for the future, and ingratitude for the present. – Osho.

Can one say that there is plenty of joy now? Excessive control, resentment, poor working conditions, lack of money, illness, dependence, disappointment, loss, and so on—all this prevents a modern person from experiencing joy. As you can see, there are a lot of reasons for this.

According to statistics, for 70% of people, the motive to experience joy, alas, is much weaker than the motive to avoid pain. As a rule, people do not go *to* something, but *from* something. They go to the doctor not in order to be healthy, but in order to stop experiencing pain. In the book "The Happiness Advantage," Shawn Achor highlights several, in my opinion, valuable thoughts on this subject.

- A large number of modern studies prove that happiness precedes material indicators of prosperity.

• When we are happy—when our state and mood is positive—then we are smarter, more motivated, and therefore more successful. Happiness is at the center, and success revolves around it.

• A positive brain has biological advantages over a brain that is in a neutral or negative state. This principle teaches how to prepare our brains to capitalize on positive emotions and increase productivity and quick wits.

Joy is one of the most important positive emotions. It lies at the heart of satisfaction, pleasure, and happiness. Joy is a positive intrinsic motivation. If we anticipate receiving joy, the action will be motivating for us.

In my experience—as a child—I was a very joyful child. I remember how I had fun and rejoiced on any occasion. At some point, the amount of inner joy began to decline. Rather, I did not even immediately pay attention to it. Life began to grow with problems, goals, and tasks. "Probably adults are not very happy," I thought. "What nonsense!" These words were literally repeated to me in the city of Denver by a wise old man whose life had been badly damaged. Five years have passed since that meeting, and I still remember his deep child-like look and a childishly sincere smile. Then he said: "If we come up with problems for ourselves, then we ourselves can come up with happiness."

In a 2004 Harvard Crimson survey, four out of five Harvard students were depressed at least once during the school year, and nearly half were so depressed that they could not function properly. This epidemic of misfortune is not unique to Harvard. At the same time, things are different in the poor village of Soweto in South Africa. Researchers visited a school located near the slums, where there is no electricity and running water. One of the researchers asked the question: "Which of those present here likes to do their homework?" It seemed to him that a universal aversion to homework would unite them. But, to his surprise, 95% of the students raised their hands and began to smile sincerely and enthusiastically.

Later, he jokingly asked the director why the children in Soweto are so weird. "They see it as a privilege," he replied. "A privilege that many of their parents do not have." (From Shawn Achor's book "The Happiness Advantage.")

Joy, Flow, Movement

In modern psychology—relating to success—one can find references to the necessity of entering a state of flow. This condition releases a huge resource and energy potential in a person. In this state, a person is able to show the highest labor efficiency in combination with satisfaction. The stream of joy that we generate begins to carry us through life, attracting the necessary circumstances for success.

Biological Cause of Joy

Joy is reflected in our body and health. This emotion is extremely beneficial, as are vitamins. When we experience joy, all organs in our body function easily and freely. In a state of joy—with deep breathing, the heart pumps blood at full strength, so oxygen and nutrients freely reach all corners of our body. The emotion of joy has a stimulating effect on our immunity, which helps to overcome diseases and even repair damaged body tissues.

Students of the medical faculty of Bar-Ilan University, along with the study of specialized disciplines, master the art of clowning. We are not talking about performances in the circus or on the stage. Future doctors are charged with the obligation to study so-called "medical clowning." Medical clowns appeared on the wards of Israeli hospitals about ten years ago. Initially, these were spontaneous performances by artists in front of sick children, but gradually the medical clowning turned into a profession. Over time, doctors began to notice that in addition to a good mood, patients improve their medical indicators and in many cases: recovery is faster than usual.

Social Reason for Joy

What happens to people when they experience the joy of communicating with each other? Naturally, they get closer, and their relationship is harmonized. If a smile appears on the face of one person, for another, it becomes a signal of a positive assessment and acceptance. Thus begins friendship, love, cooperation. Usually, people are not attracted to stern people and moody people, unless, of course, they have what you really need.

In addition, a smile tells a person that you are all right. You are healthy, happy, and successful. A joyful person attracts attention and causes a desire to communicate with them. This is an important component for establishing business relations. A seller who does not know how to smile will never achieve great success in trading.

At the same time, joy is a powerful motivator for achieving goals. The emotion of joy is a welcome prize that a person will be able to receive when he reaches a certain result. If joy is not expected, then the desire to achieve the goal is usually small. That is why the combination of "joy of the process" and "joy of the result" gives the person the highest motivation. This is the state of the stream.

Esoteric Reason of Joy

Joy must be shared; by sharing it, you relieve yourself of the burden. When you share it, new sources open up in you, new streams run. This desire to share joy is love. Thus, one thing must be remembered: you cannot love until you have joy. – Osho

Since the emotion of joy is one of seven basic emotions, its conditional age is about 50 million years. And this means that it was still inherent in our ancestors. Naturally, such powerful energy, enclosed in the emotion of joy, had its foundation in religious and esoteric sources. According to Slavic chronicles, the word joy consists of parts of "Ra" and "access", each of which is endowed with a special meaning.

"Ra" is the sun god in ancient cultures.

"Access" comes from "give," "get," and " wealth."

Our ancestors attributed the emotions of joy to the Divine nature, and staying in this emotion was an important component of serving the higher powers. Joy from the "good news" and the joy of serving God were often seen as the main features of Christianity.

Pleasure, Happiness, and Joy

Pleasure is physiological; joy is psychological. Pleasure has a bodily, animal nature. Joy is more subtle. We can say that pleasure is the lower level of joy, and joy is the highest level of pleasure.

When we are hungry, the absorption of food gives us pleasure but does not necessarily cause joy. If you dine at your favorite restaurant, eat your favorite dish, then your pleasure will probably be very great. If at the same time, you are surrounded by pleasant company, then this circumstance and the related events can cause you joy.

The Benefits of the Emotion of Joy

In order to increase the amount of joy in each day, there must be a good reason. Indeed, any change must be profitable.

Benefit No. 1: Feeling joy, we become more confident in ourselves.

Benefit No. 2: Feeling joy, we add meaning to life and the feeling that we do not live in vain.

Benefit No. 3: Feeling joy, we feel necessary and desirable.

Benefit No. 4: Feeling joy, we are satisfied with ourselves and the world.

Benefit No. 5: Feeling joy, we experience strength and are ready to overcome any difficulties.

Benefit No. 6: Feeling joy, we focus on the positive qualities of a person.

Benefit No. 7: Feeling joy, we feel a deep connection with the world.

Benefit No. 8: Feeling joy, we add life to our every day.

Benefit No. 9: Feeling joy, we improve our health and well-being.

Benefit No. 10: Feeling joy, we truly enjoy and admire the world.

Joke: Scientists have found that the orange color releases emotions, boosts self-esteem, and is an excellent antidepressant. A bill of 100 USD has the same emotion boosting properties.

Joy Management

In order for joy to arise, there are two ways to encourage joy:

Method 1 – Allow joy in yourself to manifest. As a rule, this is achieved by the practice of various meditations, in which it is possible to stop the internal flow of thoughts.

Formulate the task of meditation, for example: "I wish to strengthen the feeling of joy in my life and strengthen determination." I ask you not to be skeptical about meditation. Once I perceived it as something alien and artificial. My experience has radically changed my attitude to meditations, and I have been practicing them in several forms several times a week for many years.

Meditation (from the Latin word "meditari") is a type of exercise that uses concentration on breathing or a mantra to clear the mind and reach a heightened state of inner calm, and for health purposes to develop control over thoughts and emotions.

Imagine yourself lying in a meadow. A lot of beautiful flowers grow around you, the cups are open toward the sun, and a light warm breeze carries their pleasant aroma. Breathe it in calmly, feel unity with the meadow, flowers, and chirping grasshoppers. Look at the blue sky with fluffy clouds, imagine yourself as light as they are, take off from the earth and swim up, up to the blue sky and the warmly shining sun. When you rise closer to the sun so that only you and the sun are in the whole sky, stop and imagine that a ray of sunlight stretches out from the sun toward you and enters the area of the solar plexus—located at the back of your upper abdomen. Let feelings of joy, optimism, vitality, and determination come within you along with the yellow-golden ray. Imagine a golden ball of light growing in the solar plexus area.

Method 2 – Create the conditions for the occurrence of joy. The famous writer Ray Bradbury found that socially-active people, whose emotional experience is very diverse, often experience positive emotions. High socioeconomic status, helping to avoid the monotony of life, also positively affects positive emotions. However, Bradbury notes that money and social status can contribute to joy, but are not able to eliminate sadness. What conclusion can be drawn from this? More events bring more reasons for joy.

If we summarize the studies of various specialists in the field of emotional intelligence and the psychology of emotions, we can distinguish a general list of joy factors:

1. Eating.

2. Interpersonal relationships and sexual relationships.

3. Debt performance.

4. Physical exercise and sports.

5. Success and social approval.

6. Application of skills.

7. Music, other forms of art.

8. Weather and nature.

9. Rest and relaxation.

10. Thoughts that loved ones or other people accept you, that they need you, that you can give something to them.

11. Thoughts on future well-being.

12. Thoughts on pleasant, happy events.

13. Thoughts about a specific person or a specific activity.

14. Thoughts on certain actions of other people.

15. Thoughts about your abilities and about your success.

16. The feeling that you are accepted, that you are needed, that you can give something to other people.

What Is Happiness?

Almost everyone begins to describe the conditions for the occurrence of happiness, and very few people talk about the emotional experience of happiness. In my opinion, happiness is a state of quiet background joy. Quiet background joy gives a clear understanding of meaningfulness, gratitude, and acceptance of everything that happens. This is the point from which you measure emotional deviations. Against the background of quiet joy, we can experience a variety of feelings, while maintaining a deep connection with ourselves and the world. It is background quiet joy, and not euphoric ecstasy, that is real happiness.

To summarize:

1. What causes joy in your daily life?

2. What trigger can trigger your joy?

3. What do you think can block the natural flow of your joy?

4. What benefits can you get from increased joy?

5. In what way, based on the information studied, do you intend to increase the amount of joy in your life?

Chapter 6: Anger Management – Emotional Resilience in Conflict

> The wisest is the one who knows how to subordinate his feelings to the dictates of reason. Both a fool and another can become angry, but a fool, blinded by anger, becomes his slave. In the heat of rage, he himself does not know what he is doing, and all his actions turn him to evil. – Egyptian proverb.

Probably no other psychological topic holds as much interest and enthusiasm as that of anger management. "You need to see a psychologist," or "Go get medical treatment!" is the usual recipe for a person who has problems with feelings of anger. But seriously, let's turn to statistics:

• According to statistics from the Ministry of Internal Affairs, 90% of murders are committed in a state of passion. This is a state in which a person is controlled by his emotions, and he does not realize what he is doing.

• According to statistics, each person spends about 10% of his life experiencing anger. Is it really the case? However, most crimes are committed precisely in the heat of passion, which is preceded by anger.

The emotion of anger is a legacy that we inherited from our ancestors. Aggression in one form or another is inherent in all animals, even in a placid pet hamster. This is the basic level of instinct that helps the mind survive, protect itself and its offspring, and undergo natural selection.

Source of Permanent Wrath

Anger is a temper, a tendency to be enraged. If a person experiences anger, this suggests that he does not satisfy some of his important needs. In the Oxford Roald Dahl dictionary, "anger" is interpreted as a destructive feeling that gives a person a lot of energy. Negative energy begins to whip over the edge, narrowing consciousness, and an adequate perception of reality. As you know, there are more than enough sources for anger in the world around us, because needs are growing rapidly, and the possibilities to satisfy them are not very good. That is why anger is a common occurrence in modern society.

Perhaps in no other state does a person feel as strong and brave as in a state of anger. In anger, a person feels that his blood is boiling, his face is burning, and his muscles are tense. A sense of self-force prompts him to rush forward to attack the offender. And the stronger his anger, the greater the need for physical action, the more powerful and energetic a person feels.

Three Causes of Anger

Anger is a consequence of unmet needs. The inner "permission" to express anger gives this emotion a "green light" to go out. Therefore, control over it is necessary from the first moment of its occurrence. I emphasize two points here: anger comes out if allowed, and control is needed from the first seconds of its occurrence.

Reason No. 1: Anger is a reaction to pain. This is a programmed reaction, which has been brought by evolution to automatism.

Reason No. 2: Anger is a continuation of primary feelings. Feelings such as fear, sadness, and guilt can be the root cause of anger.

Reason No. 3: Anger is a consequence of the assessment given to a situation. If you define a situation as unfair or contrary to your values, anger arises.

The Positive Function of Anger

Because unmet needs are the cause of anger, anger helps to satisfy those needs. That is, anger is the release of emotional energy in order to mobilize a person to achieve a result.

For example, in my experience, I become very angry when I am hungry. For a long time, I could not forgive myself for this, but after talking with other people, I realized that this is a common condition. Now I am sure that a person experiencing hunger becomes enraged, and this is normal. This anger was necessary for our ancestors in order to go hunting and get food for themselves and their families. Another point is that this energy in the modern world is not as demanded as that of our ancestors. The world has become different, and we need to learn how to direct this energy into a constructive channel. Personally, now I always have something to eat at hand.

Five Rules for Anger Management

"Anger is the beginning of madness." – Marcus Tullius Cicero.

The issue of anger management is a matter of having the right beliefs and tools to help regulate this feeling. If anger is "swallowed," it transforms into resentment, irritation, apathy, and other negative feelings. Psychosomatic diseases such as hypertension or diabetes mellitus, two of the most common diseases associated with suppressing anger, can also occur. Therefore, suppressing anger or swallowing it is not the most useful way to interact with it.

Rule number 1 – Decide to take control of your anger.

Accepting it, you give a signal to your unconscious to learn how to cope with this emotion. At a conscious level, you acknowledge the fact that you cannot cope with anger and need help.

Rule number 2 – Strengthen your self-esteem.

Regard any attack in your direction with interest as useful information for thought. Exercising is an excellent prevention, thanks to which you learn to endure pain and take a blow.

Rule number 3 – Learn to recognize the harbingers of anger.

These are beacons that signal that you are entering a danger zone for you. Watch yourself when you are annoyed. It can be tension in the abdomen, increased heart rate, tightened jaws, etc.

Rule number 4 – Learn to reinterpret the events that happen to you.

If you interpret the situation as a threat, disrespect, or injustice, anger will automatically turn on. The important thing is not what happens to us, but how we interpret it.

Rule number 5 – Reduce your expectations from those around you.

Try to tell yourself more often that other people are not here in order to meet your expectations. A large number of problems stem from our belief that everything should be the way we want it; and immediately. Together with you on this planet lives another seven billion people, and this fact must be taken into account.

Anger Management Technology

In my experience, during some training that was dedicated to working with anger and rage. One of the participants said that the rage overwhelms him entirely, and he becomes unable to control himself. He recently got out of the car and kicked in the side window with a driver who "cut" his car off at a bend. He understands that such a reaction is abnormal and can lead to sad consequences for him and others. We began to investigate this issue and came to discuss his beliefs. It turns out that his dominant value is: justice. He imposes a filter of "justice" in all spheres of life and is guided by it, using himself as a guide. He secretly assigned himself the function of guardian and defender of justice. Every time, in his opinion, justice is violated, a huge dose of energy is spilled into his body to restore the broken truth.

Step number 1 – Acknowledge to yourself that you are angry. Realizing the emotion, we take control of it. Unconscious emotion begins to control us.

Step number 2 – Stop for ten seconds! Take a few deep breaths. This simple method will help relieve tension and restore breathing. Anger tends to increase breathing pace. And if it is not stopped at the initial stage of "irritation," then it will be very difficult to do so. As a result of the "stop," you get valuable time to make the right decision in the situation.

Step number 3 – Put yourself in the place of the person who caused you anger. Managing anger is, in many ways, the art of compassion. Try to understand the other person's position and behavior sincerely. The basis of any action is a positive motive. The desire to understand and accept where another person is coming from helps you to feel compassion. Compassion gives you an emotional advantage and confidence.

Step number 4 – Now think about the best solution in this situation. Ask yourself: what is the best solution and action now? What result do I want to get with this reaction? Sometimes humor and an appropriate joke will help defuse the situation.

Step number 5 – Suggest a solution or take action. Be as aware as possible in the moment. Do not give in to possible provocations and emotional attacks in your direction. You have taken control of anger, and now you need to keep it in a controlled framework. Speak calmly and confidently. This will strengthen your control over anger and weaken the anger of the other interlocutor.

I have bad news: aggression in relationships will still continue. What has been forming for millions of years will not immediately disappear. Disruptions will certainly occur, but less and less often. Do not rush and do not reproach yourself for failures. Many people have radically changed their lives, having learned only three or four of the anger management techniques I described, including myself. And you can.

And now the good news: we can develop meta-attention and learn to weaken instinctive reactions, replacing them with humanized ways of behavior.

To summarize:

1. What problems do you usually experience because of uncontrollable anger?

2. What triggers your anger?

3. What methods of controlling your anger have you tried?

4. Which of the five rules described above caused the greatest response in you?

5. Which of the five anger management steps will be easy for you, and which ones will have to be worked on?

Chapter 7: Managing Fear, and How to Develop Courage

> Fear is the mind-killer. Fear is the little-death that brings total obliteration. I will face my fear. I will permit it to pass over me and through me. And when it has gone past I will turn the inner eye to see its path. Where the fear has gone there will be nothing. Only I will remain. – Frank Herbert.

Do you think life is possible without fear?

Fear is one of the seven basic emotions; it has a retaining function and is based on the instinct of self-preservation. However, when this fear begins to dominate other emotions, it makes it difficult to do things and generally enjoy life. At this moment, it's not you, but your fears that are the masters of life.

If you look at a detailed medical guide, you can find about 500 varieties of phobias that are diagnosed as mental disorders. At the heart of all forms of fear is the fear of death. Phobias are exaggerated fears that are not based on common sense. According to various sources, about 9% of the planet's population over 18 suffers from various phobias.

The source of basic fears and concerns originates in childhood. At birth, we are just functioning on instinct, with vulnerable bodies and an undeveloped brain. In childhood, we are much influenced, our confidence is insufficient, and self-esteem is based on the opinion of older people. The period up to seven years of age is the most important for the formation of beliefs, which we then have to live with all our lives. It is here that the basic foundation of fear is laid.

Fear Management

In 1949, Egas Moniz received the Nobel Prize for his work in the field of physiology and medicine related to a lobotomy. He found that removing the prefrontal lobe of the brain robs a person of fear. However, this area has a special function: it helps us present possible scenarios. This discovery made it possible to realize that our fears are caused by the ability to visualize the future mentally. Thanks to this, we foresee the possible dangers and ultimately realize that one day we will die. From this, Egas Moniz concluded that not thinking about the future means lessening one's anxiety.

Even when we are not afraid, we may be haunted by the expectation of a possible threat, which also causes fear. And getting out of this vicious circle is not so simple. This is the reason that most people live as if they will never die, but die as if they never lived.

Caution—the following is a list of emotional triggers that can undermine your sense of inner security:

1. The world is full of dangers.

2. People are evil and dangerous.

3. People want to hurt and harm me.

4. People want to use me for their own purposes.

5. If I'm not on the alert all the time, people will be able to use me and harm me.

6. I cannot protect myself.

7. I cannot take care of myself.

8. I cannot resist the pressures other people place on me.

9. I am afraid to say no.

10. I always expect something terrible to happen to me.

Did you recognize something that you think? If so, do not rush to justify yourself. Be patient a little more, until the final questions at the end of this training.

Anecdote: Every normal person should have fears carried from childhood. Otherwise, psychologists will be left without work.

Only when you are face-to-face with fear, can you defeat it. In all other cases, fear becomes a winner. Our task is to subjugate fear to ourselves and put it at the service of our goals. Recognizing your fear is not a weakness. It is courage. I believe that the fear of recognizing and voicing our fear is one of the reasons that we are driving it to a subconscious level.

Sense of Inner Security

A sense of security arises mainly from within. Unfortunately, most people are convinced that security is something external. For a long time, we all believed that material aspects are synonyms of security: a lot of money, constant and reliable work, stable relationships, and so on.

Your real security is an unshakable knowledge: no matter what happens, you yourself have everything you need to fulfill all your wishes and to transform for the better anything that is undesirable, taking into account all your true needs. As a result, you always maintain confidence and trust, because you know: there is always a solution to everything.

In order to learn how to cope with fear, it is not at all necessary to deeply analyze its cause. This will further aggravate the situation. Quite the contrary, it is necessary to focus on the polar feeling—namely, the development of courage. Fear and courage are reactions that a person can and must control. Courage is the same skill as any other. It can be developed by systematically working on your fears and using special techniques to increase courage.

I have conducted several fear management training programs. And in my experience, every time, I saw the same script. Adult uncles and aunts carry children's fears within themselves. The method that I often use is working with the body. The fact is that all fears settle in our body in the form of bodily "clamps." When we find these clamps, and with the help of special exercises, we knead them.

Fear must be visualized, described—how it looks, how it attached itself to the psyche. Further, it is necessary to say goodbye to this fear. One of the participants said "goodbye" to their fear of a crowd of people. To do this, right at the training, we created a crowd of people for him, each of whom spoke his name. This group metaphor helped him to see himself as an integral part of society, to accept his community with people, and the value of contact.

Technology of Courage

Joke: As a child, I was afraid of the dark. Now, when I see my electricity bill, I am afraid of the light.

Step number 1 – Accept your fear. One must accept the idea that fear is a natural reaction to a new or potentially dangerous action. Tell yourself: "Yes, I'm scared now!" This way, you can take your fear under primary control and stop its development.

Step number 2 – Ask yourself three questions:

1. Why is this fear harmful to me?

2. How is this fear useful to me?

3. What will be my reward if I overcome this fear?

Step number 3 – Make a decision to overcome your fear. Where there is confidence and determination, fear recedes. You need to know firmly why you need to overcome your fear.

Step number 4 – Train your courage. First, write down on a piece of paper all that you are afraid of, then:

• Divide these fears into three categories: strong, medium, and weak.

• Identify which fears on this list are good for you and which are bad.

• Start by overcoming weak and harmful fears. The useful ones do not need to be touched; we need them for survival.

• Face your weak and harmful fears every day. Track this feeling in yourself and take action to overcome it. Even a small advance is already a victory!

• After overcoming fear, thank yourself for this victory.

Gradually, as in the gym, increasing the weight of the dumbbell, you will learn to overcome more powerful and harmful fears. As a result of such work, you develop inner courage and a sense of emotional security. Courage is not the absence of fear; it is the mental strength to withstand fear and persevere.

To summarize:

1. Which of the proposed emotional triggers of fear are yours?

2. What is the function of fear in your life?

3. What limitations as the result of fear have you encountered?

4. What can stop you from developing courage?

5. What will help you to develop courage?

Chapter 8: Self-Confidence – The Path from Uncertain Self-Esteem to Reliable Self-Worth

> If a person does not have self-confidence, he does not trust anyone in this world. While developing self-confidence, he gradually reveals that trust. This often depends on relationships with those whom he begins to trust. One who does not believe in himself does not believe in others. – Hazrat Inayat Khan.

What about your self-confidence? How often do you feel confident throughout the day?

• According to statistics, about 34% of people are extremely insecure, and 58% of the population in certain situations feel some doubt, hesitation, and confusion.

• Only 8% of people in the world really know what they want and how to achieve it. So if you are among the last 8%, I congratulate you wholeheartedly, while the rest will have to work on themselves to change their lives for the better.

The topic of increasing self-confidence is a fairly frequent request for training work or individual consultation, and my experience says that age does not matter here. I had a client who was already over 50, and he was very unsure of himself as a man. His whole life was filled with situations of avoiding fear and insecure behavior in the most crucial moments. This deprived him of many opportunities and prevented the achievement of goals. Even for a consultation, he did not dare to come for a long time. He said that he was tired of living at half strength and finally decided to "breathe life" in full.

Psychology of Confidence

Our brain is constantly evaluating the situation. From these assessments, our beliefs are formed that guide our behavior. I like comparing beliefs with programs and drivers on a computer. Depending on what programs are installed, it will impact the functionality and performance you get on the computer.

Confident behavior is beneficial for many reasons. According to Charles Darwin, in the animal kingdom, confident behavior means that smaller creatures will often outperform those of a larger size. Confidence demonstrates superiority and strength. Confident behavior disarms the opponent, giving him doubt, fear, or even panic. As a result, more confident individuals receive more material wealth and therefore become more viable. This is a natural selection.

The famous scientist, psychologist Alfred Adler believed that the basis of a person's life struggle is not sex, as Freud claimed, but rather a sense of inferiority and dysfunction, which are inherent in everyone. This is the central core of uncertainty. Adler believed that a child, small and helpless, inevitably considers himself inferior in comparison with the adults around him. By the way, he experienced all this personally from his own experience in childhood.

Indeed, a child does not have enough experience to form an accurate picture of themselves. Therefore, in their assessment, they focus on the opinion and reaction of adults. That is why proper education is the foundation for a successful and prosperous person.

Speaking of confidence, it is worth dividing this concept into several interconnected feelings and conditions. Often these concepts are confused, thereby depriving a person of the opportunity to choose adequate methods of development.

Self-Confidence

At a certain age, self-confidence is necessary for a person so that they can determine the limits of their capabilities. Self-confident behavior can give short-term success, but in the long run, it is losing that triggers an emotional swing: "I am shit." How many people swing on this swing daily? According to my observations, there are many such people in the creative environment.

Self-confidence is a recognition of the absence of a person's disadvantages and an exaggeration of one's own capabilities. It forces a person to take unjustified risks, take on tasks that he naturally might not be able to perform. He also publicly declares this to the whole world. I always watch with interest the interviews and press conferences of boxers before they fight. Some of them simply splash with self-confidence. And after losing, their disappointment and emotional decline is pronounced! At the basis of self-confidence, of course, lies a deep sense of uncertainty, which was formed in a person in childhood.

If the mother, during the first year, was engaged with the child only by necessity (and in this case, the development of the child's walking skill means the end of infancy) this can impact them greatly. As the child begins to crawl and not to be at rest for a minute, poking their nose everywhere, the punishments become more severe and frequent. And spontaneous bruises and injuries occur more often. If the feeling of rejection does not soften during the second year of life, the child concludes: "Something is wrong with me." In this situation, the development of the "inner adult" is hindered.

Summing up, we can say that self-confidence serves as compensation for past failures or low self-esteem or acts as a means of protection from a sense of vulnerability.

If the assessment of one's personal abilities is incorrect, then decisions—and as a result, human actions—can lead to defeat, which can lower self-esteem. Conversely, if the assessment is carried out correctly, the likelihood of success and self-esteem increases.

In other words, self-esteem is a constant process of comparing oneself and one's actions with some kind of internal ideal (standard) as well as good contact with internal and external reality. This ideal can both really exist and be a figment of fantasy. Self-esteem is the most vulnerable and protected category. Many people are content to close it away, like hiding jewelry in a bank safe. But does this solve the problem? Unfortunately, only partially. You can always find someone who, with a crowbar, "breaks the safe" and tramples your valuables.

Piggybank of Confidence

Records of the troubles kept by the "inner child" cannot be erased through a volitional decision. What can be done is to start accumulating records that determine the favorable results of our actions.

Accumulating positive experiences, we form a state of sustained self-confidence. Imagine this in the form of a piggy bank. This condition needs constant confirmation and success. Drop by drop you build your confidence potential. The final point in the development of confidence is self-worth, or "invulnerable self-esteem," which no longer needs confirmation and does not require approval from others. This is a "fireproof amount" that is with you for the rest of your life and can never be spent under any circumstances. Self-confidence is a necessary condition for happiness and success.

Self-esteem is tied to specific indicators, with which a comparison takes place. Positive experience to increase self-confidence is formed in four main areas of life, which is defined as "a balanced model of human development." These are:

1. The body.

2. Activities.

3. Contacts (family, friends).

4. The inner world (senses, fantasies, future).

Each of these four areas is a vital pillar that either adds confidence or takes it away.

What is confidence coming from the body? Health, attractiveness, nutrition, physical pleasures, recognition of others, strength, endurance.

What is confidence coming from activities? Results of activity, favorite business, money, career, status, recognition, success, achievements.

What is confidence coming from contacts? Love, care, attention of relatives and friends, spending time together, replenishing the family, traditions.

What is confidence coming from the inner world (senses, fantasies, future)? Positive thoughts about the future, inner freedom, dreams, spirituality and strength of mind, personal growth, beliefs, religion, and principles.

Investment in Your Confidence

Each of us is an investor. Even if there is no money, everyone invests their time and attention in something. Even just watching TV, we make a kind of investment. If we invest our time and attention in each of these areas, the result is reliable supports that add energy, the desire to live and move on. Even if a crisis occurs in one of the pillars, we become able to safely get out of it at the expense of other pillars.

Task: Pillars of Self-Confidence

Take for 100% the total amount of your energy and attention. Now distribute this percentage into the just mentioned four areas, based on how you live now. If in one of the areas you get 10% or less, this should serve as an alarm bell for you. This is a risk zone, with problems that can lead to a decrease in your overall self-confidence. In this case, make a specific decision that will increase the percentage and restore the balance.

From Self-Esteem to Self-Worth

> A diamond that has fallen into the mud is still a diamond, and the dust that has risen to heaven remains dust. – Chinese proverb.

The highest level of confidence is self-worth. Unlike confidence or self-esteem, self-worth does not need proof. Self-worth is a position, not a feeling. Self-worth is a stable sense of self—regardless of any negative circumstances that occur with a person. As a rule, people with stable self-worth perceive other people in the same way. At the heart of self-worth lies the concept of "value." Value as a characteristic of an object, meaning recognition of its

significance. Significance and usefulness are not inherent in them by nature but are subjective assessments of specific properties. For example, a 100-dollar bill may be an ordinary piece of paper for a resident of some African tribes. Or the message that came to you by mistake by email, which you deleted, carries crucial information for another person.

My good friend and colleague Tatiana conducted training on intrinsic value, in which I asked a client couple to take part in. At this training, she shared her findings, and this prompted me to a whole layer of awareness and decisions, based on what gave people value:

1. Communication with parents.

2. Partnership.

3. Close friendship.

4. Communication with the "clan."

5. Favorite business.

6. Nature.

7. Motherhood/fatherhood.

8. Mission.

9. Belief in something (e.g. religion).

These sources add meaning to life and provide a sense of self-worth and well-being. Each of these sources reflects an internal value, upon contact with which a person is filled with energy and inner calm. By establishing contact with each of these sources, we maintain our self-worth in a stable and reliable position. I am sure that each of us has contact with each of these sources. In this case, the quality of this contact is important. Perhaps, for a full flow of power and energy, we need to take out the stones with which these sources are littered. I call "stones" our beliefs, resentments, anger, fears, and much more.

Assignment: Declaration of Self-Worth

Studying the topic of intrinsic value, I came across a study of the famous American psychotherapist Virginia Satir. This declaration forms your perception of yourself and increases self-confidence. This should be done regularly, preferably every morning. I will give only an excerpt from this declaration, but, in my opinion, it can already add this state of inner self-worth to your life.

> I am me. In the whole world there is no one else exactly like me. Everything that comes out of me is authentically mine ... I own my fantasies, my dreams, my hopes, my fears – I own all

my triumphs and successes, all my failures and mistakes ... I can see, hear, feel, think, say, and do. I have the tools to survive, to be close to others, to be productive, and to make sense and order out of the world of people and things outside of me – I own me, and therefore I can engineer me – I am me and I AM OKAY. (Satir, 1975)

Task: Increasing Self-Worth

Put a score in front of each source of self-worth, where one is the minimum indicator, and ten is the maximum. This is to show the level of your contact with each source:

1. Communication with parents.

2. Partnership.

3. Close friendship.

4. Communication with the "clan."

5. Favorite business.

6. Nature.

7. Motherhood/fatherhood.

8. Mission.

9. Belief in something (e.g. religion).

After self-assessment, make a decision for yourself on the sources with which you set the lowest score. Identify specific actions you will take to increase contact with a particular value.

To summarize:

1. What sources of self-worth and self-confidence do you need to develop?

2. How and when will you begin to do this?

3. What will be your first step toward developing your confidence and self-worth?

4. What are the benefits of developing confidence?

Chapter 9: Laughter Anatomy – How to Develop a Sense of Humor

A good sense of humor has always been appreciated in society. Humor brings people together, relieves tension in communication, and gives the owner of good humor the strength to overcome difficulties. Sometimes it seems to me that I am the owner of this feeling, but there are times when I feel that it has left me. But one thing I know for sure: when I experience it, life becomes easier and more interesting.

The research company Ipsos-Reid interviewed residents of ten countries to find out what qualities they consider most important among members of the opposite sex. For residents of most of the countries surveyed, the most important thing they looked for in a representative of the opposite sex is a sense of humor.

In my experience, one situation in particular made me think about the importance of this feeling in life. I noticed the great demand for humor in entertainment now. Humorous programs have the highest ratings on radio and television. Concerts of comedians gather audiences in the same-size halls as hip-hop stars. People, like butterflies, fly into the light: go for positive emotions. And for this, they are willing to pay money. Humor has become a commodity that sells well. Usually, people buy what is needed and what is missing. Demand for humor is always high, especially in difficult times, and it is a means of emotional nourishment.

A sense of humor is the ability to relate to what is happening with ease, make humorous comments or behave in a funny way in some situations. Humor helps you find oddities in your environment, enjoy them, and better adapt to life.

The comedian Jim Carrey said: "Steve Jobs was an amazing person. He will live in my hard drive forever!"

The inherent ability to detect errors and inconsistencies and to focus on finding ridiculous and funny things in everyday surroundings—this is the basis of a sense of humor. Look around you, and with a great desire, you can find such inconsistencies. For example, you are reading this book now, although you must do some important work at this time. Funny, is it not?

Laughter is an innate reaction. A newborn baby already in the third month of life begins to smile. The biological significance of smile and laughter is to inform parents that their child is full, healthy, and satisfied. There is an opinion that according to the laughter of a person, you can determine who is in front of you. An open and loud laugh is inherent in a confident, open, and strong personality. A restrained chuckle speaks of a person's uncertainty or his hidden fears. Therefore, if everything is fine with you, nothing prevents your open and loud laugh.

Seven Functions of Humor

In the old days, fishermen took jokers, comedians, and songwriters with them to the sea. They were given the same share as all fishermen, although they did not catch fish. They entertained the fishermen in their difficult, dangerous, monotonous, and mentally stressful life on a tight ship and thereby prevented quarrels and even mental illness. Such people were called "holiday men."

Function number 1 – Humor as a way to improve health. Laughter increases the level of energy in the body and thus heals a person. No wonder they say that one minute of laughter adds five minutes of life. The "laughing body" activates about 80 muscles. Other than that, laughter:

• Increases the flow of oxygen to the brain.

• Reduces physical pain.

• Reduces blood pressure.

• Strengthens the immune system.

• Trains the heart.

• Ventilates the lungs.

Function number 2 – Humor as a psychological defense. The ability to laugh at oneself is an indicator of a person's mental health. Most fanatics and terrorists are very serious people. Such "seriousness" turns into intolerance and hatred toward people around them, and as a result—toward oneself.

Function number 3 – Humor as a way of psychological attack. In discussions or negotiations, we can, with the help of humor, devalue the cunning arguments of an opponent, if the logical arguments are powerless.

Laughter inflicts painful blows to an enemy, and makes them lose confidence in their abilities and, in any case, makes the enemy's impotence obvious ... Sarcasm is to humiliate the enemy by turning what he considers serious into the insignificant.

Function number 4 – Humor as a way to cope with life's difficulties. First, you need to distance yourself from the situation and see its funny side. The ability to relate to oneself and one's life difficulties with humor presupposes the presence of other important qualities, such as optimism, confidence, self-criticism, and creativity.

Function number 5 – A sense of humor helps smooth out conflict situations. Self-irony or irony about the situation expressed correctly and appropriately, helps defuse the situation. If there is an opportunity to experience positive emotions, people instinctively use this opportunity. Thus, relevant humor is a great emotional shock absorber for conflicts. "A smile is a curve that straightens a lot," said Marilyn Monroe. There have been many cases in my life when it was humor that was the golden key that opened the door to a person's heart.

Function number 6 – Humor as a way to build trust. Witty joke, humor, cheerful mood—all this can help us to establish positive and trusting relationships with a specific person and even with a whole group of people.

Function number 7 – Humor as a way of emotional self-regulation. Probably the most affordable way to immediately uplift ourselves to a positive emotional state is laughter therapy. Laughter gives an emotional shake to the body and fills it with energy. As a result, after five minutes of laughter, breathing deepens, the body is enriched with oxygen, the heart rate calms down, blood pressure decreases, the body is released from the stress hormone—adrenaline. Laughter has an analgesic effect: ten minutes of laughter is replaced by a morphine injection.

Technology for Developing a Sense of Humor

A sense of humor can and should be developed. Some believe that this is a gift that nature has awarded to humans. At the same time, now entire workshops of comedians are working on the creation of humorous programs, to supply artists with new jokes. I want to share one of these "technologies" with you now:

Step number 1 – The first thing to do is to decide to treat yourself without undue seriousness. Look for what may seem funny in yourself. If you are ready, you can get this information from your friends or relatives. These may be features of your appearance or character traits, etc. Tell other people comic stories from your life. Do not be afraid to laugh at yourself. This will make you emotionally invulnerable.

Step number 2 – You need to increase your vocabulary. Reading books, listening to speeches, lectures, participating in training, you will significantly increase your vocabulary. Try to introduce new words into your speech, as a result of which your humor will become more refined, accurate, and beautiful.

Step number 3 – Develop associative thinking. Choose any object that caught your eye, then start writing down the associations that come to mind. Try to bring your associative thinking to the point where words come out easily and without much thought.

Step number 4 – Try to find inconsistencies in the world and emphasize them. For example, see how the sun shines, and it can be cold; you went to the country to rest while working there as a handyman; or the official receives a small salary while driving an expensive car.

Step number 5 – The joke must be understood.

To do this, spy on successful techniques from famous comedians, try various combinations, playing with voice, pauses, casting, intonation, jargon, etc, because the wittiest joke delivered poorly and at the wrong time, can be perceived as a flat remark.

To summarize the training:

1. What function of humor turned out to be the most valuable for you and why?

2. How can the use of the information received affect your life?

3. Which of the steps in developing humor will be easy for you? And what additional efforts will have to be spent?

4. Give ten examples of inconsistencies that you observe in the world and which can be translated into humor.

Chapter 10: Sorrow – The Antidote for Depression

> If sadness has come to you, the old woman in black, do not drive her away. Plant her next to you and listen to what she wants to tell you. - Carl Jung.

The emotion of sadness and related feelings and conditions are very relevant for many people. An abundance of information, a fast pace of life and a constant race, fast food, and "one-time" relationships—all this affects our emotional well-being. Having given this emotion enough attention and understanding its mechanics, you can learn to release the great potential of energy inherent in it.

Emotional discomfort is suppressed by various narcotic drugs, which have become part of many cultures. At the same time, the title "Psychologist of the Year" was again won by "Vodka!" Not a bright prospect, is it?

The World Health Organization (WHO) compares depression with an epidemic that has spread throughout humanity: it is one of the most common mental disorders—more than 350 million people from all age groups suffer from it. Half of those people suffering from depression do not seek medical help at all, and of the remaining half, only 25-30% go to see a psychotherapist. In some countries, the number of those who do not seek medical care is approaching 90%.

Between 45 and 60% of all suicides on the planet are committed by patients with depression. According to forecasts, in 2020, it is depression that will become the number one killer. In addition, the emotion of sadness serves as a powerful accumulator of emotional energy. Sorrow, like a bowstring, can pull our intention, and later shoot a dizzying lift and success.

In my experience, during training or individual consultations, clients do not immediately present the topic of sadness or depression. In society, it is customary to hush up such emotional problems. One girl told me that of all the feelings she experiences throughout the day, sadness takes up about 50% of the time. This is a very large percentage. At the same time, she says that for her, this is a normal condition and she does not imagine how it could be otherwise. As a result of working with sadness, this girl learned to manage the great energy that lies behind it. It turned out that she was a very talented poet and directed all of her potential into creativity by publishing several collections of poems.

Celebrities who have experienced sadness and depression:

- Winston Churchill. The famous British Prime Minister of the Second World War was pursued all his life by the "black dog"—severe depression. The fact is that Churchill gave a nickname to his blues. He says that depression was the "companion" of his life.

- JK Rowling. The author of the Harry Potter novels thought about suicide when she broke up with her first husband. After the divorce, all her thoughts were about how to get out of poverty and put her daughter on her feet.

- Hugh Laurie. Recently, the actor admitted that he suffered from depression from adolescence and constantly struggled with it, but did not even show it.

- Jim Carrey. Another depressive comedian on our list. In an interview in the 60 Minutes program, Carrey admitted that for many years, he felt like his hero from the movie "Mask." On the set, he grimaced and grimaced, and when he came home, he swallowed antidepressants from constant longing. However, shortly after his visit to a psychotherapist, Carrey admitted that "problems need to be solved, not washed down with pills," he went in for sports and even promised to write a book about his fight against depression.

The Role of "The Victim"—Sadness as a Lifestyle

Our suffering is nothing more than our own habit of suffering. For some, it is developed to a greater extent; for others, to a lesser extent. For some people "suffering," is a lifestyle; for others, it is a way to survive another crisis.

My experience: in consultation with one of my clients, I was faced with the fact that he did not want to take responsibility for his life and his results. He constantly found reasons why everyone around him was to blame for his problems and failures. When I supported him, it made the situation even worse. Therefore, I decided to change the strategy and confront him more in matters of responsibility. This has brought positive results. We managed to reach the inner position of the "victim," which originates in childhood. The client himself was shocked, realizing the reasons for his behavior.

Answer the question: "Do you play a 'victim's' script from childhood?"

Constantly test yourself for the role of the victim. Do you often feel like a "victim?" Do you have the feeling that you are unfairly offended or deprived? Maybe you think that you were born to the wrong parents, in the wrong country, or even at the wrong time? A person with a victim's philosophy has been collecting evidence of this since childhood. At one time, I myself was such a collector. My childhood, like the childhood of many children who survived the collapse of the Soviet Union, passed in a survival mode.

Sadness as a Resource

As noted by scientists C. Costello and C. Izard:

> Sadness, slowing the overall pace of a person's life, gives him the opportunity to 'look back.' Slowing mental and bodily processes that accompany the emotion of sadness allows you to take a fresh look at the world, see it differently, and set other priorities in your life, which is difficult to do in the conditions of the daily routine. This new perspective may exacerbate sadness, but it can also refresh the outlook on things, which will allow us to understand what we have not thought about before.

From this point of view, sadness can be very helpful. Of course, many people are not very pleased to experience this emotion. It can appear suddenly, along with some memories of something that can't be changed. However, there is also a bright, pleasant sadness. I especially love to experience it in the fall, when the activity of nature slows down and, stopping, it reaps the fruits of its rapid development. By entering into resonance with nature, one can experience deep contact with their own values, thereby refreshing their perception of the present and future.

Three Solutions That can Permanently Relieve Chronic Sadness

Every day, we make thousands of decisions. Some decisions make us think and resort to analysis; others are taken quickly or spontaneously. There are solutions that benefit us, and there are those that do harm. I propose for you to take these three decisions right now that will permanently save you from chronic sadness:

Decision number 1 – Say to yourself, "The sadness that I am now in is temporary!" Successful people see problems as something temporary, while losers believe that there will be no end to their failures and sorrows. On the ring of the wise King Solomon was written, "And this will pass ...," which means that everything in this world is temporary. This is a very important awareness because it is because of this that you have a resource of hope, patience, and acceptance that will add strength during periods of sadness.

Decision number 2 – This feeling has a reason; otherwise it would not have come. These causes are vulnerabilities in our psyche. They tell us what we should pay attention to, since the strength of the whole chain is determined by the strength of the weakest link. If the situation repeats itself from time to time, this indicates "harmful beliefs" that once played an important role for us in the past, but are now preventing us from moving forward toward our success and happiness.

Decision number 3 – Sadness came so that I could change my life for the better. To change a person's behavior in a given situation, it needs to be given a different meaning and significance. In particular, to develop emotional stability during a stressful situation, it is necessary to reduce the significance of this situation. It is also helpful to have a "positive interpretation" of the situation. For example, in the morning, a friend of mine discovered his car without wheels. The first thought that occurred to him after a second of shocked surprise was: "Thank you for taking the old wheels that would have probably killed me!"

To summarize:

1. How much percentage of your total emotional state for a week is sadness?

2. What is the main reason for your sadness?

3. What triggers your sadness?

4. What is the belief behind your sadness?

5. What steps do you intend to take to reduce the level of sadness in your life?

Chapter 11: Inspiration – Where Is Your Enthusiasm "Start" Button?

"You can do anything if you have enthusiasm." – Henry Ford.

Everyone has situations when work needs to be done, but inspiration does not come. Sometimes, however, the lack of inspiration justifies one's inaction, right? No inspiration, why strain then?! In such cases, it is useful to have the "start button" on hand, which is guaranteed to launch action. If the result is necessary, everyone begins to resort to their own and proven—but not always useful—ways to start the inspiration. As Alexander Pushkin said, "Inspiration is the ability to bring oneself into working condition."

No matter what was done with inspiration—it could be cooking dinner or painting a fence, creating a picture, or writing a report—if the work is done with inspiration, it is felt and positively reflected in the quality of its execution.

According to the data provided by Business Magazine in 2012, the average enthusiastic employees (75%) demonstrate the highest enthusiasm in the first months of work in the company. But after three months, this figure drops by 15%. In other words, after three months of work, the employee shows clear signs of disappointment. They usually reach a critical point after three years, when they lose on average up to 19% of their former enthusiasm. At this moment, the level of his involvement is reduced to 56%, and the employee is ready to dismiss and seek a new job.

Approximately, the same situation occurs with increasing wages. Studies of Frederic Herzberg's theory of motivation have shown that higher wages increase work enthusiasm for a period of three to five months. In the future, the employee gets used to their new level of income, and this ceases to influence their involvement and motivation.

In addition to my practice in the field of EQ, I have been working as a business coach for sales and services in various organizations for a long time. In my experience, a feature of many salespeople is a low level of enthusiasm for work. That is, for the first six months they "burn," and then something happens. Indifference to the results, and fatigue from communication with customers—all this is observed in most sellers. After the training, the situation usually changes, and they will "dig the ground with their hoof" again and want to run to the clients quickly. Over time, even the request to me changed to: "Shake them properly!" Or: "Inspire the desire to work in them!" I am not a magician, but I am sure that the inspiration of the participants in my training is one of the reasons for which business trainers love their work.

Nature of Inspiration

Initially, the word "enthusiasm" denoted the condition of a person possessed by a deity or under his influence. Indeed, it is very likely that in a state of inspiration, we become "obsessed" with some kind of idea or process. This is a mental upsurge, with creativity and labor excitement, manifesting in the ultimate mobilization of all spiritual and physical forces.

Sigmund Freud said: "When inspiration does not come to me, I go halfway to meet it."

According to my observations, people with good mental organization have a frequent influx of inspiration. A period of concentration replaces a state of impotence. Often, I see people of a creative appearance, walking alone in a park and pointlessly kicking leaves on the ground or feeding swans in a lake. Enthusiasm can embrace them anytime, anywhere, or maybe not come for months.

With inspiration, you can perform any work, both creative and physical. If the work is done with inspiration, the "breath" will be felt everywhere. The very concept of inspiration is very closely associated with breathing: inhale-exhale-inhale-exhale.

Inhaling—we receive energy; exhaling—we give it away. Hence, the derivatives: inspired and exhausted. Pay attention to your breath in a state of inspiration. You practically do not breathe, and the lungs burst with pleasure. Oxygen is fuel for inspiration at the body level.

In Chinese philosophy, "breathing" also means "energy," the general name for "Chi." It is a life force that permeates and unites all that exists. Chi fills each of us; it makes our blood run through the veins, makes our breasts breathe, and thanks to it, all phenomena in nature occur.

In addition to saturating the body with oxygen, you also need a feeling of inspiration and the right mental orientation. The feeling that underlies inspiration is interest, and mental orientation sets an important goal or value. The combination of all three components gives a special energy chord, which is called "enthusiasm" or "inspiration."

Ten Triggers – Killers of Inspiration

Since we are talking about subtle spiritual energies, any external or internal stimulus can bring down these sensitive alpha waves, and in their place will come apathy, irritation, boredom, and so on.

In my experience, one of my clients complained that during the period when he needed to write a Ph.D. thesis, his neighbor was training as a boxer. The punching bag sounds drove him crazy, and he could not concentrate on work. Moreover, he could only work at home, and the neighbor did not go into any negotiations. The seemingly hopeless situation was resolved very simply. We identified ten places suitable for work and took turns experimenting. As a result, the most productive place for him was an underground cafe in town. Now, it is his favorite place for creativity.

Killer number 1 – Situations with the balance of "Take-Give." This is when you do not get emotional strokes or recognition from the people for whom you tried.

Killer number 2 – Situations when you do work or perform actions that do not reflect your inner values and aspirations. In this case, you realize that you do not live your life or do your job the way you want to.

Killer number 3 – Situations in which you are constantly absorbed in your work, not switching to other areas of life. In this case, there is an emotional burnout, satiety, and even aversion to work.

Killer number 4 – Any situation that brings you out of balance. When you experience feelings such as envy, jealousy, fear, guilt, etc., these are funnels that suck in your emotional energy.

Killer number 5 – Situations in which you are in a "victim" state. Here, you feel your vulnerability and the inability to influence events.

Killer number 6 – Incomplete situations, unfinished business, significantly reducing enthusiasm. Incompleteness draws upon itself energy that could be used here and now.

Killer number 7 – You make impossible promises and take on too much responsibility. You can make a hasty decision, and then feel a decline in emotional strength.

Killer number 8 – Fear of criticism. The constant fear that someone will negatively evaluate your result.

Killer number 9 – Inability to get satisfaction from the result. Satisfaction is an emotional reward for achievement. She is a powerful internal motivator for action and achieving goals.

Killer number 10 – Several failures in a row that reduce the level of self-esteem, and, consequently, enthusiasm rapidly falls. Constant failures without extracting a lesson from them put pressure on a person and leads them to a state of hopelessness.

As you can see, ten killer triggers "hunt" our enthusiasm, making this state vulnerable. No wonder we rarely experience it. In order to protect it, I advise you to adhere to the following recommendations:

Enthusiastic Launch Technology

Once, when I was a student, I worked as a loader in a cosmetics warehouse. It was an evening job, and my duties included packing orders. After several months of monotonous work, and especially in the pre-holiday periods, when there were especially many orders, I invented my own way of maintaining enthusiasm. From orders, I formed entire fortress cities on the floor. Each package was a brick building. And in the morning, when sales representatives came to collect their order, they were waiting for a new surprise. They said that they did not even want to disassemble these works of design thought.

Step number 1 – Change the situation for a while. New places give rise to new impressions, new thoughts, which increase inspiration and enthusiasm for work.

Step number 2 – Breathe deeply for ten minutes, which will help saturate the body with oxygen.

Step number 3 – Mentally connect the upcoming work with your life goals and values. Find meaning in your every business. An aimless pastime discharges the batteries of your enthusiasm. It is useful to have a set of triggers that will allow you to trigger the necessary emotion.

Step number 4 – Think about what element of creativity you can bring to the upcoming work. In each seemingly routine task, you can find something unusual that will cause an emotion of interest. By stimulating a sense of interest, you influence your inspiration.

Step number 5 – Start any business with gratitude for the opportunity to be useful to someone and fulfill oneself. When you go beyond your ego in your work, you have additional energy.

To summarize:

1. How often do you feel enthusiastic?

2. Which of the killer triggers preys on your enthusiasm?

3. What can trigger your enthusiasm?

4. Under what circumstances does enthusiasm usually occur in you?

5. What benefit does enthusiasm give you, and what would change if you had more?

6. Which of the proposed recommendations did you immediately want to implement?

Chapter 12: Infected with a Sense of Guilt

"Beware of those who want to impute guilt for you, for they crave power over you." – Vaslav Nijinsky.

The ability to feel guilty is common to all people. This deep anchor was formed in the process of human evolution. The central fear of the culprit is the fear of being rejected by society, of losing all benefits. As a result, they would experience death from physical and emotional hunger.

Feeling "guilty"—a negatively colored feeling, the object of which is your act, which, in your opinion, is the cause of negative consequences for other people. Guilt is the price we pay for violating certain standards of conduct or beliefs. As long as our behavior is beyond these standards, guilt will not cease to haunt us on the heels. This program is embedded in the social DNA of our society and is passed down from generation to generation.

According to British analysts: almost all women—namely 96%—feel guilty every day. Nearly 80% of adults who have ever attempted suicide suffer from chronic guilt or shame. Twenty-five percent of children aged three to fourteen "punish" themselves for masturbation or for the fact that in their thoughts they wanted someone to die. Ten percent of people can independently cope with their feelings of guilt, the remaining 90% either suppress it or resort to the help of a priest or a psychotherapist.

In my experience, the topic of guilt is a request included in the top-ten requests that people make when working in a training session or at individual consultations on managing emotions. And it is not always the issue that is immediately obvious. At one of these consultations, the client complained of frequent bouts of unexplained anxiety. He said that it appeared suddenly and then also suddenly disappeared. When we started exploring this topic, it turned out that he felt guilty of how he spends his time. It turns out that in childhood, his father constantly shamed him for his idleness. According to the parent, the son had to do something useful constantly. Subsequently, this trigger program formed the basis of his life scenario. And now, in those periods when he is not busy with anything, the voice from the past gives him a feeling of guilt, which manifests itself in the form of sudden anxiety.

The accusation has such a strong emotional effect that it is very difficult to resist it while maintaining internal balance. The accusative tone gives rise to guilt, fear, or anger in another person. Therefore, realizing this strong influence, many people use it to achieve their goals. For example, the grandmother blames the mother, then the mother blames the father, then the father blames the son, then the son blames the friend, and so on, to infinity.

Feelings of guilt are imposed on a person from childhood. Parents often shame or scold the child for not eating porridge, for soaked rompers or for a broken toy. Constantly shaming and punishing the child, they teach him to feel guilty.

Even animals are capable of feeling guilty. While there is no scientific evidence that some animals actually feel guilty, their facial expressions and behavior allow you to compare them with people who experience the same emotions. Several times I saw dogs and cats that behaved guilty when the owners shamed them or scolded them for some misconduct. But do animals that live away from humans feel guilty? Is guilt a purely human emotion, or is it inherent in other animals? We have yet to get an answer to these questions.

Joke: A husband who returns from a business trip admits to his wife that he has lost his engagement ring.

"I don't understand," the wife is indignant, "how can one manage to lose their ring?"

"You are to blame for this! I've been telling you for a year now that my pocket is torn!"

Double-Edged Sword

The internal standard that guides human behavior is conscience. Conscience is a person's need to be responsible for their actions. Conscience is based on empathy as a mechanism of the social instinct for the conservation of the species. Braking mechanisms against harming a member of a pack or population exist in many animals. In human society, due to the ambiguous understanding of harm, conscience is overgrown with educated moral standards.

Feeling guilty is a double-edged sword. As soon as you feel guilty, at that very moment, you have learned to evoke it in other people. And many people have succeeded significantly. I would say that they became the owners of the black belt in this kind of "sport." Living with this feeling is unbearable; however, there are many meanings in it, and removing it we will destroy the structure of our society. If you manage to get rid of this feeling, know that this structure will collapse in the first place, because you have no idea how much it means to you. The only question is: what will come in its place?

Ten Basic Forms of Guilt

I found an interesting gradation of forms of guilt with the famous American motivational speaker Anthony Robbins. It would seem, why should the motivational speaker, who professes to know the psychology of success, collect and study this material? I am sure that the guilt of many people is an obstacle to success and happiness. Different types of guilt are colossal hatches for taking our psychic energy. They suck out whole kilowatts of energy from our emotional reservoir, which we could direct to achieve results. Therefore, first of all, I propose to diagnose the types of guilt that you have and take them under initial control.

What kind of emotional trigger activates your guilt?

In this task, you need to determine on a ten-point scale that you have one of ten types of guilt. Put in front of each a number, where one is the minimum value, and ten is the maximum.

1. Parents/Child. Parents, through evoking feelings of guilt, carry out educational work. Performed a task one way—you're good! Performed it another way—you're bad! A child idealizes the parents, so their assessment is an deeply felt.

2. Child/Parents. Children, unable to negotiate with their parents, learn to arouse guilt in them so that they fulfill their whims. Also, the child, due to guilty feelings, can repay unpaid debts to his parents all his life.

3. Supervisor/Subordinate. The same laws apply as between parents and children. The prototype of the boss is the "imperious parent."

4. Teacher/Student. The same laws apply as between parents and children. The prototype of a teacher is the "imperious parent."

5. Love. Manipulation of love is used by partners to achieve their goals. "If you love me, do ... If you don't, then you don't love me."

6. Legislative. There are vowels and unspoken rules in society. These regulators are composed of ethical standards of

conduct and civil laws (constitution). These prescribed rules ensure the functioning of society. Prison is an excellent example of law enforcement.

7. Sexual. The sexual theme in society is taboo. Only in the last 30 years did the curtain of secrecy rise and people have begun to try to speak openly about it. This has been formed for more than a thousand years and is one of the criteria that distinguishes us from animals. Many people are so infected with this guilt that they completely reject bodily intimacy and sexuality in their relationships.

8. Religious. The original sin is a form of control over believers. You were born and were already to be blamed before the eyes of God.

> The first man fell in paradise, and that the sin spread from here, successively to all offspring so that there is no one born in the flesh who would be free from that burden and not feel the effect of a fall in real life. (Message of the Patriarchs of the Eastern Catholic Church on the Orthodox Faith.)

9. Self-stacking. This is a fictitious fault that we impose on ourselves, satisfying the inner scenario. Guilty without guilt. We are to blame for being alive and well, for a relative to die, a natural disaster, a plane crash, and so on.

10. Existential. The great sages of Rishi affirm that we all have basic obligations—a duty to our ancestors, the earth, our mentors, God, all those who have ever helped us. When this debt remains unpaid, we suffer from a sense of existential guilt.

How to Get Rid of Guilt?

A participant in one of my training courses could not forgive herself for the death of her mother. She believed that her mother died through her fault due, to the fact that she did not pay enough attention to her. During the consultation, it turned out that her guilt (and the feeling of responsibility) is a special form of pride! Say,

"This world revolves around me, and it depends only on me who lives and who dies."

In fact, we cannot be held responsible for the choice of another person. Only for the consequences of our own choices! The death of another person, no matter how strange it may sound, is the result of their choice, even if unconscious. If you could determine which type of feeling you are infected with, please accept my congratulations. This is already 50% success. Guilt is so tightly fused with the structure of the psyche that a person becomes compressed with it and ceases to separate it from himself. Guilt is a parasite that is in a kind of symbiosis with the human psyche.

The next step is the process of letting go of guilt. You must be able to say goodbye to guilt and catch it in the early stages in the future so that it does not take root.

According to Irvin Yalom, professor of psychiatry at Stanford University:

> Neurotic guilt comes from imaginary crimes (or petty misconduct that provokes a disproportionately strong reaction) against another person, ancient and modern taboos, or parental and social prohibitions. The "genuine" guilt is caused by a real crime in relation to another person.

Is it possible to get rid of it once and for all? I think that this is impossible. This program (trigger) has already been deeply imbedded for many thousands of years of human development. But we can learn in time to diagnose useful or toxic (neurotic) guilt, as well as to manage it, reducing its intensity and impact on us.

Step number 1 – Is there really your fault in what happened? Separate real evidence from your illusions. If you are not sure, describe the situation to people you trust, find out other points of view.

Step number 2 – Admit that you feel guilty. With gratitude for the valuable experience, acknowledge your guilt. Guilt signals a violation of your personal emotional standard.

Step number 3 – Evaluate the trigger. Then evaluate whether the violated standard is worthy of preservation. Is it good for you and others? What function does it perform? If this standard is destructive and is not useful to you, you need to abandon it. You can analyze which trigger fires and what form of guilt arises. Then select a new useful trigger and concentrate on it. If necessary, write it down and scroll it several times a day in your head, introducing new scenarios of behavior. Take responsibility for the consequences.

Step number 4 – If what happened is your fault, ask for forgiveness. Forgiveness is an important ritual to let go of guilt. In the Christian tradition, there is even a "Forgiveness Sunday" before Lent. Arrogance or ordinary fear may interfere with asking for forgiveness. If these feelings are really a problem, work them out using the mental training in point number three.

Step number 5 – Separate this feeling from yourself. You are … and there is your guilt. Explore this feeling: how it looks, how it is reflected in the body. This step will help you distance yourself from it.

Step number 6 – Determine the value touched by guilt. Which of your values are affected by this situation.

Step number 7 – Find a positive side in the situation for yourself. In any act lies the positive intention of the person who commits this act. What was your positive intention in this situation?

Step number 8 – Draw conclusions based on the current situation. Decide not to allow a similar situation in the future.

Step number 9 – Forgive yourself for this act. There are no ideal people; people tend to make mistakes. This situation is an important lesson in your life. Repentance releases accumulated tension and makes the heart easier.

Guilt will go away, but what will come in its place?

Guilt will be replaced by personal responsibility for the consequences of your actions.

Responsibility is a future orientation that builds on lessons learned. This is a perception of oneself as an adult and holistic personality, who is aware of the connection between their actions and the results obtained, and they readily accept both positive and negative consequences of their actions.

Sometimes my clients ask me what a mature person is? In my opinion, responsibility is one of the criteria of a mentally healthy and mature person. And responsibility is not just like a yoke on the neck, which tires you and makes you unhappy. On the contrary, it is useful to be grateful for the responsibility of the trust placed and the opportunity to be useful and necessary. This is a manifestation of your maturity. This is a topic of value and meaning. And what is the meaning of responsibility for you?

To summarize:

1. Which form of guilt do you experience more often than others?
2. In what cases do you decide to cause guilt in other people?
3. Is the guilt you feel useful or toxic to you?
4. What triggers your guilt?
5. What will change in your life if guilt becomes less?
6. What will change in your life if feelings of guilt become greater?

Chapter 13: Anatomy of the Feeling of Resentment – The Recipe for Radical Forgiveness

"As soon as you learn to be offended, that very second, not the next, but that very second, you will learn to offend." – Anonymous.

Resentment is one of the types of racket feelings with which we "extort" attention, respect, care, remorse, and so on, from the offender. This is a way to punish the offender so that he changes his attitude to something, repents and realizes that he was wrong.

My experience: at the beginning of a relationship with my wife, she often resented my behavior. Yes, and I often noticed that I am harsh in answers when they catch me at the "inappropriate" moment, although I never had a conscious desire to offend. This caused us great trouble, as she was often offended, and I, considering this to be nothing, did not always ask her for forgiveness. She did not see another way to influence my behavior. In principle, this is a classic option for many couples. After several months of such insults, we were tired of it, and we decided to develop a new model of behavior. She insisted in immediately pronouncing her feelings at the time that a "touchy" situation arose. This method served as a wonderful discharge and reduced the number of mutual insults to a minimum.

The word "resentment" comes from the word "cheat," and therefore it is closely related to such a thing as: justice. We are offended when we consider that a person is being unfair in their treatment of us. The scope of this feeling can also be different. There may be a slight momentary resentment, or there may be a lifelong resentment.

Resentment is an emotional funnel that is addictive. We scroll again and again in the head offensive situations. Resentment builds up in the heart and at some point, it can develop into anger or even hatred. And in parallel with this, from childhood, we learn to forgive, sometimes replacing real forgiveness with pseudo-forgiveness.

Research in the field of medicine has established that our body instantly responds to a grievance with muscle tension, and the stronger our emotional state, the stronger the muscle clamp. First of all, resentment delivers a blow to the throat and chest—this is the confirmation of the saying "stifles resentment." Over time, negative cases are forgotten, but leave an imprint on health, disrupting blood circulation in constricted muscles. Thus, immunity is reduced, and an impetus is given to the development of serious diseases—such as heart attack, bronchial asthma, and coronary heart disease.

What can cause resentment? *Anything.* Nevertheless, the most common causes of resentment are:

1. Insults.

2. Taunts.

3. An accusation.

4. A threat.

5. Ignoring a request.

6. Causing physical pain.

7. Deception.

8. Humiliation.

9. Disappointment.

10. Add your favorite …

Each of these situations trigger this feeling, and can be interpreted as offensive.

Anatomy of Resentment

Touchiness is a manifestation of a child's ego state. That is, we can be 30 or even 50 years old, but inside we can feel like a five-year-old scared child. It is this inner-wounded child who very often makes decisions, gives out emotional outbursts, especially when a "sore spot" is stepped on.

Joke: Offended by my husband, I decided not to talk to him. But something tells me that I didn't scare him, but inspired hope in him!

At the heart of this feeling are unjustified expectations, or more precisely, the mismatch of our expectations with the real behavior of a significant person. When, for example, the one from whom you expect support or praise suddenly starts criticizing or reproaching you, you feel a blow to self-esteem, you feel that you are being treated unfairly and are offended. A reaction to such a situation could be an outburst of anger, but such behavior is not welcomed, because you do not want to pass for a quick-tempered person who does not know how to control your emotions (besides being openly angry with relatives or your boss.) But you can always squeeze your lips, keep silent and take offense.

Dangerous Resentment

Resentment is dangerous—primarily for ourselves. Why? Because we, again and again, scroll through this situation in our heads. Resentment accumulates in the heart, and every day, a person rekindles it in himself more and more. In this case, resentment can develop into anger or even hatred. The situation that caused it is overgrown with more and more pains and speculation. As a result, resentment spoils our mood and in the long run, negatively affects our physical and emotional health.

In my experience, one of my clients has been resenting his peer for 20 years, because he was greatly humiliated by him at school. All his actions were dictated by a plan of revenge. Even his success in life was achieved as a response to the bullying to which he was subjected. And the fact that his offender is no longer alive did not remove the offense because it became a "psychological spine" for his personality, the main meaning of life, without which he did not know how to live on.

If it seems to you that resentment is a strong step and an opportunity to save your self-esteem, then you are mistaken!

Quite the contrary, resentment speaks of your vulnerability and psychological dependence on others. It narrows our consciousness to the size of the offender, increases irritability, breeds hatred, and revenge. In my opinion, a psychologically mature person is not offended. They may decide to break up, for various reasons, but will only do so for the good of both parties. And what is the point? Resentment is an incomplete situation. Rather, it is the ellipsis behind which lies the distant hope of renewed contact. This hope of restoring justice in some very expressive and memorable way—ideally, the other side should draw conclusions, and even better—strongly regret what happened is harmful and unrealistic.

Pseudo Forgiveness

How many insults have you forgiven in life? And how many of these grievances have you completely let go? I want to say that "forgive" and "let go of an insult" are two different concepts. According to my observations, pseudo-forgiveness is a very common occurrence. Resentment researcher Colin Tipping even identifies several types of pseudo-forgiveness:

- Forgiveness from a sense of duty. We think forgiveness is the right and even spiritual thing. We believe we must forgive.

- Forgiveness from a sense of righteousness. If a person forgives people because he believes that he is right and righteous, and they are stupid or sinful, and he pities them, this is pure arrogance.

- Fake forgiveness. Pretending that you are not angry for any reason when you are really angry, you are not so much forgiving as you are repressing your anger. This is a form of self-denial.

Even if you "forgave" your partner, this does not mean that your resentment has been erased from memory. Grievances accumulate until their critical mass is reached. After which, there is an emotional discharge in the form of a quarrel or, conversely, depression. When this will happen, no one can predict.

Sometimes the slightest reason is enough for an "explosion" to occur, which in its power is not comparable with the cause. Sometimes in the course of such an emotional breakdown, insults of many years ago, about which everyone has already forgotten, begin to be extracted from the memory. If the grudge is not responded to, a person can maintain their emotional charge for many years: like mines from World War II, waiting in the wings.

Pseudo-forgiveness comes more from politeness. It's easier for many people to pretend that they have forgiven than to truly and completely let go of their grievances. Really letting go of a grudge can be disadvantageous. In order to really forgive completely, it is necessary to use special techniques. My experience shows that relying only on logical arguments and solutions for forgiveness is not enough. What can I say if in my practice, I often meet people who hold a grudge against people who are no longer alive? Where is the logic here?

Forgiveness Technology

Based on my experience, I concluded that most often, people who carry a grudge are women (or at least, they are more open about it.) Sorry if I offended someone. At one training session, a woman told her story in which she could not forgive her husband for a long time because he once slapped her in the face. From that moment on, she built a psychological barrier around herself and did not let it go. That is, formally everything was as before, except for real closeness and openness. Seven years passed after that incident, their children grew up, and she continued to hold the inner-defense system. Her husband, who had been feeling guilty all this time, was recently diagnosed with cancer. When she found out about this, something broke in her. From that moment, she began to give him all the accumulated tenderness and love that she had held back for so many years. Their relationship has never been so intense, close, and open, as it is now.

Step number 1 – The first thing to do is to admit that you are offended. Having voiced this for yourself, you will take this feeling under your control and acknowledge the fact of its existence. Do not blame yourself for this feeling. Resentment happened, and now it is a starting point for your further actions. Write down why you were offended, and by whom.

Step number 2 – Do not make decisions in a state of resentment. "Take your hand off the fire." You need to take a break, which "dampens" hot emotions, and you can make decisions with a calmer mind. Determine how much time you spend on your grudge.

Step number 3 – Determine what your expectations regarding this person are that did not materialize. What kind of emotional trigger worked? Unjustified expectations underlie resentment. Describe your expectations regarding the behavior of the person with you. Answer the question: "Why should they behave the way I want?" Here is your trigger, which triggers a sense of resentment. By putting forward your unspoken claims on others, you will fall into your own trap when your expectations are not met. Learn to lower your level of claim on other people, and you will immediately notice that the amount of resentment in your life will decrease.

Step number 4 – Try not to evaluate the behavior of a person in relation to you. Often people commit their actions unintentionally, without setting themselves the goal of offending. Ultimately, what matters is not what is happening to us, but how we react to it! Sometimes, only after years, one can understand what a positive role a person's actions toward us was, even if at that moment, it seemed unjust and offensive. Look at the situation from a broad spiritual perspective—from the world of Divine Truth. We ourselves created this situation in order to learn from it a valuable lesson for ourselves. Obviously, the stronger a person is involved in a situation, the more difficult it is for him to see a benefit for himself in it.

Step number 5 – Develop a dialogue ability about resentment. Do not carry it for long in yourself, pretending to be dejected, so that the offender himself guesses and, feeling guilty, apologizes to you. This creates an imaginary advantage for yourself. In fact, carrying this "toxic" feeling in you, you spoil your mood, destroy your spiritual harmony, increasing anger, and revenge.

If something is really important to you, it is necessary to pronounce and conclude verbal agreements. In this case, expectations are transferred to the category of responsibility. If there is no way to discuss the situation with a person, write him a letter. However, sending this letter is not necessary. In any case, if you do, this will relieve your stress, and you can calmly look at this situation.

Step number 6 – Practice forgiveness. This is the main recipe against resentment. Forgiving sincerely and deeply, letting go of the situation, you unload your psyche, getting rid of the severity of resentment. This does not mean that you are forgetting the situation. To draw conclusions, to learn, to mark your vulnerabilities—this is the benefit that you can learn from this feeling.

Mantra for the Offended:

In the end, here is an exercise from the Osho master—"Mantra for the offended." After reading it, pass through his conversion and realize the futility and weakness of this feeling.

> I'm such an important turkey that I can't allow anyone to act according to their nature if I don't like it. I am such an important turkey that if someone said or didn't do what I expected, I will punish him with my insult.
>
> Oh, let him see how important this is—my insult, let him receive it as a punishment for his "misconduct." After all, I am a very, very important turkey!
>
> I do not value my life. I do not appreciate my life so much that I do not mind spending precious time on resentment. I will give up a minute of joy, a minute of happiness, a minute of playfulness; I would rather give this minute to my insult. And I don't care that these frequent minutes add up to hours, hours—to days, days—to weeks, weeks—to months, and months—to years. I do not mind spending the years of my life offended—because I do not value my life. I do not know how to look at myself from the side. I am very vulnerable. I am so vulnerable that I have to guard my territory and respond with resentment to everyone who touched it. I'll put a "Caution, Angry Dog" sign on my forehead and let someone try not to notice it!
>
> I am so poor that I can't find in myself a drop of generosity to forgive; a drop of self-irony to laugh; a drop of generosity not to notice; a drop of wisdom not to catch; a drop of love to accept. I'm a very, very important turkey!

To summarize:

1. What are you usually offended by?

2. What benefits do you derive from resentment?

3. What triggers a grudge?

4. What can you do now to reduce resentment in life?

5. Who do you need to forgive first?

6. How and when will you forgive him (or her)?

Chapter 14: Jealousy

"Looking at how some accumulate good, others begin to accumulate evil." – Anonymous.

Have you ever been jealous? I will assume, yes. This feeling is inherent in all people. It underlies competition and the ability to survive. At an early age, we envy older children because they are taller, stronger, and more allowed to participate in sports. At school, we envy certain students because they have more freedom and already know who they want to be. If you are a bachelor, then you envy married people, and if you are married, you envy single people. Having no money, you envy the rich. And those who have money envy those who have power. And this process is endless.

The feeling of envy is a feeling that is associated with the desire to redistribute some good in the person's own favor. This is one of the forms of aggression, but in a milder form. The source of envy is unmet needs. The leading driver of envy is the position about the unfair distribution of resources in the past and/or present.

But there is another side. From a positive point of view, "white" envy is the ability to acutely realize one's needs and desires through the achievements of other people. That is, if we envy someone, this can be a motivating factor for self-development and achievement.

When does envy appear?

If we have everything we need as far as: supplies of food, water, air, sleep, housing, and safety, as well as (and this is important) at least part of what those around us have—basic needs do not bother us. At the same time, dissatisfaction with basic needs is experienced rather hard. Immediately there is self-pity: so what is it—"Everyone had lunch, and I'm hungry, like an orphan?" And the more natural we consider our need, the stronger the pity: "Everyone is asleep, I sit alone and finish the work at midnight, that's such a sorrow."

For envy, special conditions must be created. These conditions, as a rule, we create for ourselves. Often this happens out of habit. Habitual behavior turns our reactions to certain events to automatism. Let's take a closer look at each of the triggers.

Envy trigger number 1 – Envy is when we compare ourselves to another person. By itself, the desire to compare oneself with another person launches a search mechanism for its (own) advantages and disadvantages. With this trigger, we will be stably provided with an object for envy. Who do you most often compare yourself to?

Envy trigger number 2 – Envy is when we compete with other people. At the heart of life, Darwin argued, is natural selection. Competition for resources for the purpose of survival and the continuation of humankind—these are the basic instincts that control our behavior. Who are you currently competing with?

Envy trigger number 3 – Envy is an admission of defeat. This is a kind of resentment against yourself when you acknowledge your imperfection. This resentment can come out in the form of anger. Remember: what we concentrate on, we strengthen in ourselves. Therefore, we can grow in ourselves even more fears, anger, or, conversely, apathy, or depression. Why are you offended by yourself now?

In addition, envy may be felt toward you. How do you feel when you know that you are the subject of another person's jealousy? Perhaps this adds confidence and a sense of emotional well-being to someone, but another effect is possible. The envy of others can cause fear. The fear of harm or, even worse, getting jinxed. Therefore, there is a category of people who do not like to spread about their successes, achievements, and joys. They live quietly rejoicing and not attracting the attention of other people.

Jealousy Management Algorithm

It is customary in society to condemn envy. In my experience, at one of my training courses, the participant proudly declared his envy for one of the World's billionaires. And it was obvious that he liked this envy. To the question: "What does this feeling give you?" He replied that it inspires and motivates him to achieve his dream. This cannot be called envy in the form in which it is usually represented. This is an example of "white" envy, which is built on a sincere admiration for the abilities and achievements of another person. We came to the conclusion that such "white" envy does not destroy a person, but, on the contrary, adds meaning and vitality. This becomes possible only if one recognizes one's own uniqueness, self-sufficiency and "okayness."

In order to translate "black" envy into "white," I propose using eight steps of transformation. Having done this task qualitatively at least once, you can rebuild your attention and place consciousness on positive energy and use envy for your own good.

Step number 1 – Admit that you are jealous. This is important to do in order to catch this feeling. Allow yourself to feel this envy; do not blame yourself for it. Often, forbidding ourselves to experience any feelings, we transfer them to an unconscious level, thereby losing control over them.

Step number 2 – Determine which envy trigger worked.

• Envy trigger number 1: Envy is when we compare ourselves with another person.

• Envy trigger number 2: Envy is when we compete with other people.

• Envy number 3: Envy is an admission of defeat.

Step number 3 – Try to remember and keep in mind what you are already successful in. Such fragments of success are necessarily in your life. Learn to rejoice and give thanks for what you already have. Switching your attention to your accomplishments can balance your attitude toward the person you envy.

Beautiful words on this subject were cited by Elena: "As soon as you begin to see the meaning in your own actions and in the current situation, self-pity evaporates somewhere, and it doesn't reach envy. The answer to the question: 'How to stop envy?' Will sound like this: 'Stop comparing yourself with others and get down to business!'"

Step number 4 – Do not be angry at your object of envy. Envy is the result of low self-esteem or lack of understanding of one's own needs. A person is not to blame for the fact that you envy them. They have paid their "price" for what they have. If you find out the details, then this "price" may be too high, and not everyone will be willing to pay it.

Step number 5 – Mentally thank this person for pointing you the way to your desires, dreams, and needs.

Step number 6 – Instead of looking for flaws in this person and condemning them, just watch their development. Learn the other person's success: What do they do and how do they do it? What led them to such results? Model acceptable models and strategies. What qualities of character or knowledge (skills) can be useful to you?

Step number 7 – Recheck yourself. Is it really important for you to have what this person has? Is it truly about you and your life? If "Yes," then act!

Step number 8 – Make a specific action plan that will help you move in the desired direction. Work with a coach if necessary.

Step number 9 – Proceed in this direction and celebrate your own successes.

To summarize:

1. Can you call yourself an envious person?

2. Which of the options for jealousy is closest to you and why?

3. What triggers your envy?

4. How do you feel when people envy you? Why exactly do you get this feeling?

5. What positive meaning do you see for yourself in envy?

Chapter 15: Poisonous Emotions

"What do you despise? By this you are truly known." – Frank Herbert, American science fiction writer.

Why is contempt considered a poisonous emotion? There are some emotions that poison a person—and those around them—when they are experienced. At first, this affects thoughts, then it switches to mood, and ends up causing physical illnesses.

In my experience, I was running a training course about emotional intelligence, and one participant spoke about his disdain for officials who were burnt on bribes. His contempt borders on hatred and was manifested in the desire to hang and shoot. It was interesting that contempt aroused in him a surge of emotional and physical energy. He seemed to be filled with strength when he spoke of another example of corruption. During the dialogue, it turned out that he did not intend to abandon this feeling completely, as he considered it adequate, but simply wanted to make it more manageable.

Nature of Contempt

At its core, contempt is a feeling of disrespect and neglect, arising in relation to a person or group of people who show certain personal qualities, commit certain actions or having certain beliefs. As a rule, a person experiencing contempt condemns these qualities and does not allow himself to show them. This feeling forms the relationship between people and creates inequality. A who person puts himself above another (according to different criteria), consciously distances himself from him.

The results of a study by the famous American psychologist Carroll Izard revealed the nature of this feeling. He believes that in an evolutionary perspective, contempt was a means of preparing a person or group of people to face danger. To put that into perspective, imagine a young man preparing for a battle with an adversary, provoking such thoughts in himself: "I am stronger than him, I am better than him." Men who adopted a similar mindset showed more courage and less empathy for the enemy.

Thus, a sense of contempt has motivational power. This means that by experiencing it, we gain additional confidence to take action.

The following variations are available. Speaking of varieties of contempt, I want you to note the sequence of its development. I am convinced that the reverse principle works here—If a man despises all of humanity, then, deep down, he despises himself:

1. Contempt for oneself.

2. Contempt for the other.

3. Contempt for a group of people.

4. Contempt for the whole nation.

5. Contempt for all of humanity.

Each of you can recall your own examples from life or history when this or that kind of contempt was manifested. For this reason, recall the contempt that the Nazis had for the Jewish race. This "imposed contempt" was so irrational in essence and rational in form, that as a result of the Nazis' actions, millions of Jews were physically destroyed. Contempt, like a virus, took over the entire German nation, making this feeling a part of propaganda ideology.

Contempt is an Intermediate Feeling

Like a surprise, the feeling of contempt is intermediate in nature, although more stable. This means that it can be an independent feeling and can go into other forms of emotion. It depends on the internal beliefs, as well as the goals of the person. The feeling of contempt can be called a "cold" feeling. Depending on the circumstances, contempt turns into:

• Anger.

• Resentment.

• Rage.

• Sadness.

• Alarm.

For example, you may experience contempt for the person who stole something, and after this feeling, anger, and the desire to severely punish the thief can instantly appear. Or contempt for the friend who deceived you, and then sadness due to the loss of the relationship.

The Emotional Benefits of Feeling Contempt

If a person does something or feels an emotion, then it is beneficial to him, even if he denies such a benefit. For a long time, I could not see this feeling from a position of benefit. However, an analysis of the scientific studies of this feeling prompted me to think about the possible benefits that it brings to our psyche. Triggers of contempt, therefore, work because they are beneficial to our psyche and fulfill an important function.

Benefit number 1 – Contempt as a sign of superiority. Having won in any business, we may experience contempt for the losing side. At the moment of contempt, we begin to feel extra strength.

Benefit number 2 – Contempt provides an opportunity to get out of the severity of our own dysfunction. Despising another, we seek an increase in our own self-esteem. Against the background of a humiliated person, we begin to rise, even if only in our own eyes.

Benefit number 3 – Contempt provides an opportunity to realize our values, beliefs, and principles. Despising, we can understand what is important to us and why. We can be proud to follow clear life guidelines that we or our environment really value.

Despite the fact that contempt has benefits, this feeling is very toxic! Highly! This feeling is subject to rapid development, like a cancerous tumor, and can go into another, even more serious condition.

How to get rid of these toxic emotions?

In my experience, one of my black friends was very contemptuous of "people of Caucasian nationality." She called them "chocks," and she was simply turned upside down when a Caucasian was next to her. Once, after her next complaint to Caucasians, who were noisy in the street, I decided to investigate her contempt with her. Answering several questions, she realized that she despised Caucasians because of their unpredictability and emotionality. This causes her fear, which she framed in the sense of contempt. "What are you afraid of?" I asked. "I'm afraid that they will rape me," she said with surprise to herself. "Why do you think they want to rape you?" I asked cautiously. "I don't know!" She answered loudly. Apparently, the cause of this deep-seated fear was the distant experience of the ancestors, who were regularly raided by alien tribes. In those days, the victorious party killed men and raped women. Perhaps the reason for this fear lies in the history of her family.

If, while studying this material, you came to the conclusion that you have more feelings of contempt than you need, and it poisons your life, then you are ready for the technique of getting rid of contempt. I note that to get rid of contempt, you must have serious motivation and a desire to get tangible benefits. These benefits should be greater than the benefits of having contempt in your life. Record these benefits right now:

Benefit number 1: _____

Benefit number 2: _____

Benefit number 3: _____

If you have identified enough benefits, we can proceed to the specific steps of deliverance.

Step number 1 – Acceptance. Accept the fact that a person's action is the best that they could (or can) do based on their life situation. We do not know in what circumstances a person is and what history they have.

Step number 2 – Understanding. Every time, try to understand the reason for the person's act, no matter how absurd it may be at first glance. Look at the situation with their eyes. Try to understand the reason for their choice. Surely this choice was well-intentioned.

Step number 3 – Uniqueness. Every time, try to see the uniqueness of the person and the experience that they bring with them. Do not compare it with any reference points and ideals. This is not easy, because you always want to compare another person with yourself.

Step number 4 – "Own price." Accept the fact: each person pays "their own price" for their actions and the lifestyle they lead. The person you despise has already paid or will pay for what they do. The price is determined not by us, but by life itself. Leave them the right to choose.

To summarize:

1. What types of contempt do you most often experience?

2. What benefits do you find in contempt?

3. What harm does this feeling do to you?

4. What triggers your contempt?

5. What feeling does your contempt usually turn into?

6. Which of the following recommendations have been most helpful to you and why?

Chapter 16: Improving Emotional Consciousness

We are motivated by emotions, not thoughts. Without an understanding of what you are feeling, it is impossible to understand your own behavior fully and, accordingly, it is neither possible to control emotions and actions, nor to read the desires and needs of others.

Emotional consciousness includes two main abilities:

1. The ability to recognize the emotional experience of the present.

2. The ability to cope with all your emotions.

These two abilities deserve our special attention.

Have you ever felt as if you were controlled by depression, anxiety, or anger? Do you, most of the time, act like you should not—by making a decision (acting, saying, or doing something,) and knowing that you will regret it later? Does it happen that you feel emotionally numb? Are you having difficulty communicating with other people and cultivating ideal standards of relationships? Do you feel that your life—the emotional "American mountains"—are solid extremes and no balance? If you answered yes to at least one of these questions, you should know that each of the described conditions is associated with a disorder in emotional consciousness.

Emotional awareness helps us:

- Recognize who we are: what we love, what we don't love, and what we need.

- Understand other people and sympathize with them.

- Communicate clearly and effectively.

- Make wise decisions based on the motives that are most important to us.

- Motivate ourselves to act to achieve a goal.

- Build strong and healthy relationships.

Emotional consciousness brings our life into balance. Those attitudes that concern almost every one of us will be replaced by others that support and approve. Compare these statements:

"When it comes to feelings, I constantly go to extremes."

"Life does not have to be constantly at the highest point; it is not only ups and downs. The more contact we maintain with our inner world, the better we control our experiences, the faster we learn to avoid extremes in reactions and experiences."

"I, most times, regret my actions and/or speech."

"If you, most times, dream about how good it would be to get into a time machine or rewind time, just not to say what you said or not to do what you did, then your path to developing emotional awareness lies through mastering patience during stress."

"I have no strength."

"When physically you are in perfect order, but you don't have the energy to force yourself to act (even if we are talking about the simplest things)—perhaps this is depression. With a better understanding of EQ, you can and will be able to reconfigure these feelings and make positive changes."

"I do not like those who like me."

"Relationships are a complex thing, but it's much easier to get to know people, make friends, and make strong connections with emotional awareness."

"I'm unlikely to succeed in life, although I'm smart and work hard."

"You already know that success in life and in work sometimes requires more than just mind and effort. Along with them, emotional intelligence is recognized as one of the leading factors for finding a better place in the sun."

"Others say that I have no feelings; they call me an insensitive person, a machine."

"There are people who do not know how to control their emotional manifestations; they are easily irritated, easily upset, and readily express what they think. But there are others: those who keep themselves under such tight control that they do not express any feelings at all. No matter what happens, it seems as if it does not touch them at all. The solution for them is to find a balance with their own feelings."

Evaluate Your Emotional Awareness

There are many tests for emotional intelligence. The vast majority of them are purely entertaining and cannot be taken seriously. You can easily distinguish such tests on the questions themselves (like: "You always feel this way when a guy likes you"). The MSCEIT test (The Mayer-Salovey-Caruso Emotional Intelligence Tests), developed on the basis of the studies of Salovey and Mayer, is considered classic. The test, consisting of one hundred and forty-one questions, gives a very detailed and reasonable result. There are other tests that you can easily find and pass if you wish. We'll dwell on express diagnostics right now.

Although emotional intelligence is the foundation of good communication, building and maintaining strong relationships, and most importantly, emotional health, people often find themselves unfamiliar with their own emotional experiences. Psychological practice shows that not many can clearly describe how they feel. The majority of people, when asked: "What do you feel?" Will answer something like: "Well, a lot, I just can't express it." And the problem is that, being unable to identify and express their own feelings, they do not even think that this is a problem. Answer the following questions; this is not a test for which you can get an assessment. But these questions will help you understand something for yourself: the more often you answer "no," the more you need to work on your emotional intelligence.

• Can you experience strong feelings, including anger, sadness, fear, disgust, joy?

• Do you feel your emotions physically? For example, if you are sad, do you have a heaviness in your chest or stomach? If you're worried, is there a lump in your throat?

• Do you ever make decisions based on intuition? Do you make decisions based on emotions?

• When your body signals that something is wrong (goosebumps running on your back, etc.), do you trust your feelings?

• Are you comfortable with all your emotions? Do you allow yourself to feel anger, sadness, or fear without judging yourself or suppressing these experiences?

• Do you pay attention to every change in your emotional state? Do you experience different emotions during the day or is the same emotion constantly holding you?

• Can you talk about your emotions?

• Do you feel that other people understand your feelings?

• When others know about your emotions, does this suit you?

- Are you sensitive to other people's emotions? Is it easy for you to put yourself in the place of another?

Most people do not know about their feelings, and even if you notice this for yourself, you always have the opportunity to fix it. By simply understanding and recognizing your emotions, and being able to manage and cope with them, you can enjoy great happiness and peace within yourself and build a better relationship.

And we repeat again: if we do not learn how to manage stress, we cannot cope with our emotions. They are not predictable, and we can never be certain for sure what will cause an emotional reaction of any type. Furthermore, under pressure, we do not seem to have the time to return immediately to a proper state. Therefore, we need tools to deal with stress quickly. The development of emotional intelligence is heavily dependent on our ability to relieve stress once it has begun. If you know how to calm down only by feeling depressed, well, that is one way and a negative one at that. Remember that emotions can help, but they can also hurt. Such fear and helplessness can lead to self-closure, inhibit your rational thinking ability, and push you to perform an action (or set of actions – verbal or non-verbal) so that you talk and do things that you will later regret.

So if emotions can contain both pluses and minuses, perhaps they can be used for their own purposes? Of course yes: even in unpleasant emotions, there is a positive note.

- Anger can be destructive and reinforcing. Out-of-control anger can run amok, endangering the person and those around them. But anger can also protect a person and save a life. Anger is an emotion that concentrates a lot of energy, and this energy can be used to save the situation, mobilizing oneself, and inspiring the right and decisive action.

- Sorrow can lead to depression, but it also supports emotional healing. Sadness encourages a person to calm down, stop thinking about the bad, be healed, and recover from the sad event.

- Fear that completely captures a person is a debilitating and negative emotion. But fear does not only this: it also activates defensive reactions that protect against external danger. Fear, deeply rooted in the soul, often causes chronic depression. Overwhelming fear can be an obstacle that separates us from others, but fear also maintains a safe life, warns of danger, and induces protective actions.

We are born with the ability to experience the full range of human emotions: joy, pride, anger, sadness, fear, and others. However, many people were disconnected from some or all of their senses. Among them, those who experienced psychological trauma in childhood often disconnect from their emotions and the physical sensations that they cause. But when we try to avoid pain and discomfort, our emotions are distorted; we lose contact with them when we seek to ignore them, rather than worry.

By evading emotions and avoiding emotional experiences:

- We refuse to know ourselves. This is one of the most important consequences: we, therefore, do not want to understand why we react to different situations in one way or another; what we want; or what we really need.

- We deprive ourselves not only of the bad, but also of the good. By deliberately turning off negative feelings: anger, fear, or sadness—we also close our ability to experience positive feelings: joy, love, and happiness.

- We are tired. Because avoiding emotions is tiring. We can distort and dull the senses, but we cannot completely eliminate them. We spend a lot of energy learning how to avoid a genuine emotional experience and keep our feelings oppressed. It devastates.

- We spoil our relationships. The more we move away from our feelings, the more we move away from other people and stop striving toward developing a pleasant social bond with them. As soon as we disconnect from those experiences that cause discomfort, we automatically disconnect from positive experiences. By such a separation, we deny ourselves joy and laughter, which, by the way, are well supported in difficult times.

Getting over losses and completing solid tasks are only possible if we can retain the ability to rejoice. This inspiring emotion always reminds us that life is worth living, and can bring not only bitterness but also joy.

What to do? Embrace and be comfortable with all of your emotions! If you have never been able to cope with pressure, the advice not to give up negative emotions may seem dubious. But, even after experiencing psychological trauma, a person can be healed, having learned how to maneuver among his emotional experiences safely. You can and should strive to change the way that you respond to your emotions. This involves reuniting with all the basic emotions, which include anger, sadness, fear, disgust, surprise, and joy, through the process of self-healing. Having set this goal and starting to implement it, you must constantly keep in mind several important points:

Emotions come and go quickly if you let them.

You may be worried that as soon as you begin to experience all the emotions you have avoided, they will stay with you forever. But this is not so. When we are not crazy about our emotions, sooner or later, even the most painful and difficult feelings subside and lose power over us. If you do not feed the emotion with your attention, you control it. You will notice that when you are at peace with your inner world, the main emotions (both positive and negative) quickly come and go. This means that during the day you see, hear, or learn something that instantly causes a strong response in feeling. But if you are not focused on this feeling, it will not take possession of you, and soon other emotions will take its place. This is the difference from the state in which you are focused intently on one particular emotion, for example, sadness; what is happening only saddens you.

The body itself will tell you what is wrong with emotions.

Emotions are closely related to physical sensations; experiencing intense excitement or joy, you feel how the body responds with tension or lightness. By taking careful note of these physical sensations, you will better understand how to manage emotions. Take for instance, there is a certain fellow that causes bitterness to appear in your mouth when you spend time with him (or her). You can conclude that it is unpleasant for you to be near him; if during a certain action your stomach contracts, then this action makes you awkward, so you don't want to do it. Of course, you yourself know perfectly well who you like and what does not suit you; but to listen to your body is useful even to a person with perfectly developed emotional intelligence because this will once again remind you of the need to protect your health.

Forget about the conflict between reason and feeling.

Let this stay only in movies and books. Emotional intelligence works like instinct. When it is highly primed, you will know how you feel like a reflex, that is, not even thinking about it; and you can use these emotional signals to understand the situation and act accordingly. The goal is not that someone wins the war between reason and feelings; the goal is to end this war and find a balance between the two participants.

Conclusion

Thank you for making it through to the end of *Emotional Intelligence: Unlock the Secrets to Boosting Your EQ, Social Skills, Charisma, Influence and Self Awareness, Including Highly Effective Communication Tips for Persuading People*. It should have been informative and provided you with all of the tools you need to improve your Emotional Quotiant and succeed in life.

Emotions are those strong invisible threads that connect people. These form the basis of understanding ourselves and establishing trusting relationships with those we need and who are dear to us.

But in order to experience all the advantages of a highly developed emotional intelligence, it is not enough just to experience emotions. You need to understand them and be able to control them. This indispensable skill can be called emotional awareness. Everything that this gives us, we don't need to get from somewhere else, we already have it. Emotional consciousness is inherent in every person; without exception—this is a feature of our species. The only difference is that some people have spent more time and labor working on its development than others. Yes, someone may have been given a high emotional intelligence from birth, but another who works on it independently can achieve the same results—sometimes, even bigger ones—because what the labor is invested in is valued more than the gift received.

Start improving your emotional intelligence, no matter how developed it is now. Humans always need something to strive for. The more emotional consciousness we possess, the more clearly and creatively we think; the easier it is to manage stress and cope with problems; and the stronger our personal relationships. Whether we know about them or not, emotions are constantly present in our environment and around our personal lives, taking a toll on everything around us. To be emotionally conscious is to know what and why we feel, to define and express our feelings, to understand what connects our feelings to our actions and to put ourselves in the shoes of others to have better, solid, positive and fruitful relationships with them.

Finally, if you found this book useful in any way, a review on Amazon is always appreciated!

Check out another book by Mark Dudley

You might like this one as well

www.ingramcontent.com/pod-product-compliance
Lightning Source LLC
Chambersburg PA
CBHW070048230426
43661CB00005B/809